WALKS IN THE
LLŶN PENINSULA
Part 1

Walks with History

Walks in the Llŷn Peninsula

Part 1
South and West

Nigel Burras and Jeff Stiff

ISBN: 0-86381-343-7

Cover: Alan Jones

*First published in 1995 by Gwasg Carreg Gwalch,
Iard yr Orsaf, Llanrwst, Gwynedd, Wales.
☎ 01492 642031*

Printed and published in Wales

Contents

Acknowledgments

We would like before we embark on these walks to express our gratitude for the valuable help and assistance given to us by the following people: Christine Stiff whose suggestion this book was, and for her assistance in proof reading and 'inputting' material into the word-processor, without her we would still be doing that now! Marjorie Woodcock for proof reading, suggestions, Welsh name translations, and some photographs. Ken Hill and Chris Kotlarz for proof reading and 'road testing' walk directions. Pete Masters for historical suggestions. Staff and photocopying machine at Caernarfon Reference Library. Especial thanks to, Edmund Hyde Hall, without whose observations this book would have been much the poorer.

It remains for us to state that any errors which may be left in the book are entirely our responsibility.

INTRODUCTION

Most of us, especially when on holiday, enjoy a good country walk, the Llŷn Peninsular abounds with them. When out walking and admiring the scenery, many of us would like to know a little of the history of any features, buildings or ancient monuments which they may come across. This book is an attempt to cater for these people, it is written by two local historians who are also avid walkers. The area featured in the following pages, is littered with features of historic interest and covers all periods from the Stone-age to the Modern.

The walks we describe vary in length and terrain to suit both the casual ambler and the dogged countryside tramper. We also bring to the attention of the reader some observations made on the area by travellers in the past, it is enlightening and often amusing to make modern-day comparisons of the area described by eye witnesses some two centuries ago. The quotes used are left unaltered and unadorned.

It may help the less historically minded amongst us, to briefly put into context the pre-historic and historic periods and their respective dates:

The Llŷn Peninsula has been home to mankind since the Palaeolithic (Paleo — 'old', lithos — 'stone') period which ended with the retreat of the last great Ice Age around 12,000—10,000 B.C.

With the end of the Ice Age began the Mesolithic (Meso — 'middle') period when groups of nomadic hunters roamed the area.

Farming came to Llŷn in the Neolithic (Neo — 'new') period, 3.500-3.000 B.C., and saw the first permanent settlements in the area.

Then follows the Bronze Age, around 1500 B.C., in this area (a little later than England).

The next period is the Iron Age or Celtic period with the first settlers arriving around 500 B.C. The Celts were by nature, a fairly aggressive and war-like race.

Then follows a long period of warring tribes & minor chieftains, glaring at each other from rival fortified hilltops.

The coming of the Romans, with the 23rd legion based at Caernarfon, tried to bring some semblance of order to the area, with limited success.

With the withdrawal of the Romans in the early 5th century, a long period ensues with more minor kings & warring tribes. This period is known in history as the 'Dark Ages'.

We then arrive at a time just after the Norman conquest of 1066, with Norman barons from the Chester area making or attempting to make inroads into north west Wales, (there are a few motte & bailey type fortifications on the Llŷn).

Then follows, in the 12th & 13th centuries, the time of the Welsh Princes and their confrontations with the English Monarchy, which culminated in the conquest of Wales by Edward I, in 1282-1283. Thus was born the county of Caernarfonshire.

There will also be from time to time in this book, references to some of the less common plants and animals that are to be found in this very special area. It is an attempt to bring local knowledge to what is already a superb area in which to walk.

Armed, as you will be, with information on where to look and find these treasures of the Llŷn, be sure as you go about your journeys to leave everything as you find it and only your footsteps as evidence of your passing.

It may at this juncture be prudent to say something about the footwear that could be comfortably worn on these walks. It is always wise when in the country to wear boots or at least walking shoes, especially when on the cliff-top paths, of which there are many in this book. It may also be of benefit to remember that although you will probably be walking in the summer, the ground can become very boggy in places. Although if this is likely to be the case you will find that it will have been mentioned, in wet weather the ground in some places can quickly become water-logged, so take care.

If you get as much enjoyment reading and walking with this

book as we did in writing it, we will have done our job and you will have gained a greater appreciation of an area that has captivated people over many centuries and for many reasons. Happy walking!

Rights of Way
A Brief Guide To The Law

1. What is a right of way?

A right of way in the countryside can be either a footpath, a bridleway or a byway. On *footpaths* the public has a right of way on foot only. Whereas on *bridleways* the public also have a right of way on horseback and pedal cycles. *Byways* are open to all classes of traffic, including motor vehicles. Legally, a public right of way is part of the Queen's highway and subject to the same protection in law as all other highways, including trunk roads.

2. What are my rights on a public right of way?

The public has a right to pass and repass along the way. You can also take with you a 'natural accompaniment', which includes a dog. However, you should ensure that dogs are under close control. On suitable paths, a 'natural accompaniment' could also include a pram or a pushchair.

3. How do I know whether a path is a public right of way or not?

The safest evidence is the definitive map of public rights of way. These maps are available for public inspection at county, district and outer London borough council offices. Some are also available for inspection in libraries and some are sold by the councils concerned. In addition, public rights of way information derived from these maps, is shown by the Ordnance Survey on its pathfinder (1:25,000) and Landranger (1:50,000) maps. But note that a path not shown on the definitive map may still be a public right of way, and application may be made to the surveying authorities for ways to be added to the definitive map.

4.How does a path become public?

In legal theory, most paths become rights of way because the owner 'dedicates' them to public use. In fact very few paths have been formally dedicated, but the law assumes that if the public uses a path without interference for upwards of 20 years then the owner intends dedication. Most public paths came about this way. But it is not true that a path can cease to be public if it is unused for 20 years (except in Scotland). The legal maxim is 'once a highway, always a highway'. Paths can also be created by agreement between local authorities and owners or by compulsory order, subject, in the case of objection, to the consent of the Secretary of State for the Environment (or for Wales).

5. What about crops growing on or over a path?

The farmer has a duty to prevent a crop (other than grass) from making the path difficult to find or follow. You have every right to walk through crops growing on or over a path, but you must stick as close as you can to its correct line. Report the problem to the highway authority: it has the power to prosecute the farmer or cut the crop and send him the bill.

6. What is an obstruction on a path?

Anything which interferes with your right to proceed along it, e.g. a barbed wire fence across the path or a heap of manure dumped on it. Dense undergrowth is not normally treated as an obstruction but is dealt with under path maintenance.

7. Can I remove an obstruction to get by?

Yes, provided that:
a) you are a bona fide traveller on the path and have not gone out for the specific purpose of moving the obstruction.
b) you remove only as much as is necessary to get through. If you can easily go round the obstruction without causing any damage, then you should do so. But report the obstruction to the highways authority.

8. What is a misleading notice?

A misleading notice is one calculated to deter you from using a public right of way, for example, a notice saying 'Private' at the point where a public footpath enters a park. Such notices should be reported immediately to the highway authority. They are illegal on paths shown on the definitive map.

9. What is trespass?

The civil tort of trespass arises from the bare fact of unauthorised entry. However, unless injury to the property can be proven, a landowner could probably only recover nominal damages by suing. But of course you might have to meet the landowner's legal costs. Thus a notice saying 'Trespassers will be prosecuted', aimed for instance at keeping you off a private drive, is usually meaningless. Prosecution could only arise if you trespass and damage property. However, under public order law, trespassing with an intention to *reside* may be a criminal offence under some circumstances. It is also sometimes a criminal offence to trespass on military training land.

Countryside code

The above stated laws represent the footpath users rights, but it should be borne in mind that when these paths cross private or farm land, you have a duty to respect the privacy and/or commercial interests in this land. For this reason we present a few points which constitute a country code which will ensure an harmonious usage between land owner and walker:

1. Please ensure that all field gates are left as you found them.

2. On a footpath through a field, always keep to the edge unless the path is clearly marked across it.

3. Make sure that you do not disturb any livestock in the field, i.e. all dogs should be kept on leads and children kept under control.

4. Take care not to trample any growing crops.

5. Do not remove any large sticks etc, from hedgerows as this could create a gap allowing livestock to escape.

6. Leave any plants and flowers where walkers after you can admire them.

7. Take all your litter away with you.

8. Help to keep all water clean, as any stream may be supplying water to households and/or livestock.

9. Guard against fire risk.

10. Don't make unnecessary noise.

11. Always keep to the designated path.

12. Always use the gates and stiles provided (hopefully!) when crossing fences, hedges or walls.

13. Please ensure when parking your car that it does not obstruct field gates etc.

Please remember when enjoying your countryside walk not to destroy the very thing you came to see.

CAR ROUTES TO WALK STARTING POINTS

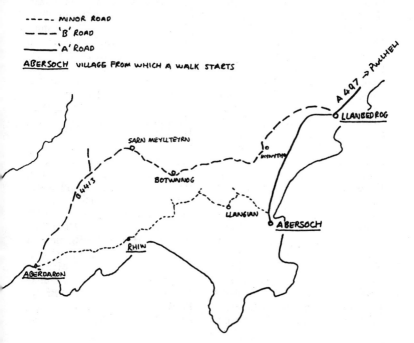

A Glossary of Welsh Names

Abaty .... Abbey
Aber..................... River-mouth
Ardal...............................District
Bach .... Small
Bangor.............Consecretal land, Monastery
Bedd .... Grave
Betws .... Prayer house, Chapel
Blaenau .... Upland
Bod............................... Abode
Bryn................................. Hill
Bwlch............................. Pass
Bychan .... Small
Caban .... Hut
Cader .... Seat, Stronghold
Cantref .... District, Hundred
Caer........................ Fort, Camp
Capel ....Chapel
Castell ....Castle
Cefn................................ Ridge
Celli................................Grove
Clas .... Mother Church
Coch .... Red
Craig............................... Crag
Crib .... Summit
Crwth .... Fiddle
Cwm .... Valley
Cymru .... Wales
Cymry........................The Welsh
Din.............................Hillfort
Dinas .... Hillfort, Town
Drwg........................Bad, Evil
Du................................. Black
Dŵr ....Water
Dyffryn .... Valley
Eglwys..........................Church
Esgob ....Bishop
Ffin .... Boundary
Ffordd ....Road
Ffridd..... Sheepwalk, high pasture
Ffynnon .... Well, Spring

Glan .... Riverbank
Glas....................... Green, Blue
Glyn.................... Glen, Valley
Gwaun..................... Upland bog
Gwely............. Bed, hence family Settlement
Gwlad .... Country
Gwyn .... White, fair
Hafod............. Summer dwelling
Hen ....Old
Hendref.... Old Township, Winter Settlement
Heol, Hewl........................Road
Is ....Below
Llan.....................Church, Place
Llanerch .... Glade
Llech .... Stone, Rock
Llyn .... Lake
Llys .... Palace Princes dwelling
Maen............................. Stone
Maes .... Open Field
Mawr .... Big, great
Melin .... Mill
Moel .... Bare hill
Morfa ....Marsh, Seashore
Myn........................ Ore, Mine
Mynachlog .... Monastery
Mynydd..................... Mountain
Nant .... Stream, Vale
Newydd .... New
Nos................................. Night
Pandy.................... Fulling Mill
Pant....................Hollow Valley
Parc .... Park
Pen.......................... Head, End
Pentref.... Hamlet, End Settlement
Perfedd .... Middle
Plas .... Hall, Mansion
Plwyf .... Parish
Pont............................. Bridge
Porth............................... Port
Pwll................................Pool

Pistyll	Waterfall
Rhaeadr	Waterfall
Rhaglaw	Government Officer
Rhiw	Hill
Rhos	Moor
Rhyd	Ford
Rhyngyll	Beadle
Sarn	Causeway
Sir	Shire
Tir	Land, Territory
Traeth	Beach, shore, stand
Traws	Cross, District
Tref	Township, Town
Tŷ	House
Ty'n Llan	Vicarage, Rectory
Uchaf	Upper
Ynys	Island
Ysbyty	Hospital
Ystad	Estate

— ROAD

---- FOOTPATH

(1) (2) etc. NUMBERS FOR HISTORICAL NOTES

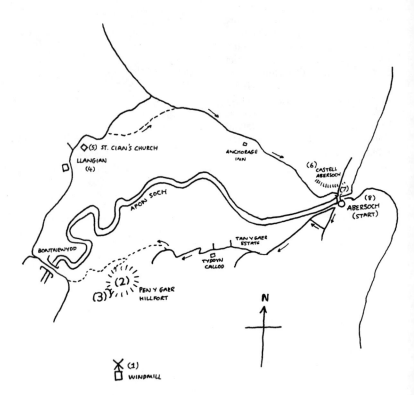

St. Cian's Church ◇(5)

LLANGIAN
(4)

ANCHORAGE
INN

(6) CASTELL
ABERSOCH

(7)

(8)
ABERSOCH
(START)

AFON SOCH

TAN Y GAER
ESTATE

BOATNEWYDD

TYDDYN
CALLOD

(2)

(3)
PEN Y GAER
HILLFORT

N

(1)
WINDMILL

16

Walk 1

Abersoch — Llangian

Two hours

The following walk is an ideal pre-lunch or pre-dinner walk and takes you through pretty scenery, passing through one of the most 'awarded' villages on Llŷn, Llangian, with its beautiful church and sheltered setting it seems a long way from the twentieth century.

A start as good as any is from the *St Tudwals*, the public house in the centre of the village. Walk up the main street until the turn off on the right. Take this road which goes past the village hall. The road is called Lôn Gwydryn (wild cape lane). At the 'T' junction at the bottom of the hill take the road signposted Llanengan heading left uphill.

The road, after a few hundred metres and another short rise, bends to the left but you carry straight on, the first house on the left after joining this road is called 'Derwyn', on the right is a sign outside a small estate called Tan-y-gaer, which is a reference to the hill fort which we will pass further up the lane, the name Tan-y-gaer means 'below the fort'.

On your left, pass a broken pine tree on a bend and there you'll observe an unusual house 'Tyddyncallod', (lungwort homestead) with what looks like a 'glass-house' on top of its pitched roof. The fort you are heading towards is visible through the trees and undergrowth, straight ahead on top of a hill. Come to a fork and take the right path through an old broken gate with the name Brongaer on it which means 'hill of the fort'. The road now runs straight for about 200 metres. Keep your eyes peeled around here for gold finches.[1]

Head towards the gate in front of you and walk straight on, keep to the wall on the left after passing through the gate. Walk on through the lane lined with gorse bushes — this is worth seeing in June. There is a valley ahead with the village of Llangian in its depth. Mynydd Rhiw is visible in the distance.

A detour is possible here, going up to the fort[2] on top of the hill. There is very little of the fort left to see, but the view from the top is worth the effort. If detouring, turn left after passing through the gate posts and head up the path to the summit, reached in a hundred and fifty metres or so.

Ramparts of Pen-y-gaer hillfort overlooking Abersoch

Retrace your steps to the gate posts and return to your route.

If you walk to the outer edge of the path in the direction of Garn Fadryn, you will see approx. 20 metres in front of you at the bottom of a grassy slope a small marshy area. This is the site of an ancient well and may have been the water source for the inhabitants of the hill fort Pen-y-gaer you have just visited.

Follow the steep track (not too steep) down the side of the hill.[3]

Ahead of you is a gate, go through this and proceed down the hillside, where, on your right is an impressive stand of reeds

(Phragmites autralis) these were used for good quality thatching, although because of its abundance locally, bracken was extensively used.

There are stone steps set in the wall bordering the road, these are visible when you are approaching the road.

Go up on to the road and turn right towards Llangian. The marshy land to the left of the road floods extensively in winter, which is why there is a bridge over this area. This bridge is called Bont Newydd which simply means 'new bridge' and divides the parishes of Llanengan and Llangian and replaced Edmund Hyde-Hall's 'bridge of three arches'. At the centre of the bridge is a plaque that tells you what vehicles may cross it and the weight restrictions — strange getting a warning when you are already halfway across the bridge! In about 200 metres you will come upon a sign post, Porth Neigwl (*Hell's Mouth*)) to left, Llangian to right in ½ mile.[4]

In a few dozen yards you will see the church of St Cian, if you have time, it is well worth a look around.[5]

On the ascent of the hill heading towards Abersoch, on the first bend, our signposted footpath breaks off the road to the right and is the way to proceed, enter through the gate into a tunnel of trees and undergrowth. Carry on to the next gate, go straight through and walk on up the slope. The view to the right is of the village of Llangian and the church yard, while beyond that stretches the wide sweep of Porth Neigwl (*Hell's Mouth Bay*). After a few hundred metres you will join the main road, turn right and follow this back into Abersoch.

Visible from the road at this point and looking right you will gain a good view of the fort visited earlier. At around this time you could well be in need of some refreshment, if so, then on your right is the 'Anchorage Inn' open all day and with some good views from the bar.

The harbour breakwater visible in the distance, built in 1924, now appears directly in front of you with the Pen Benar headland behind it. Follow the road for approx. ¼ of a mile and then you will be entering Abersoch. When you reach the village and the main road, on your left there is a garage and boat salesroom, called 'Abersoch Land & Sea'.[6] Turn right here and head back into the village centre.

On your left as you walk along the main road is an area known as the 'Green' but is in fact filled with sea water at high tide, this is the winter resting place of many of the local boats. At low water look out for the resident heron, fishing for the many eels which abound in this river.[7],[8]

Just before reaching the village centre are public toilets on your left.

History notes

[1] On your left, just visible through the trees and about two fields away is the remains of an old windmill. This would have been the place where the inhabitants of Llanengan would have brought their corn, etc, to be milled by the resident miller for the cost of a few pence. This mill was already in a ruinous condition by the early 1800s.

[2] On arriving at the summit take in the scenery for a few minutes. The fort itself is of oval structure, the remains of the entrance lies to the north east. This fort was occupied by a wave of Iron Age settlers sometime around 100 B.C. It should be thought of not as a fort, but more as a fortified hamlet or family settlement. It was thought to contain two stone-built round huts, together accommodating no more than 12 to 20 people. It may have been one large family or a couple of smaller families that had united as a 'tribe'. The occupants would have been agriculturalists growing cereal-type crops. They would probably have had a few cows and sheep and maybe goats. With the close proximity of the sea they would undoubtedly have supplemented their diet with fresh fish.

It was probably the Romans who put an end to the occupation of this site. The 23rd Legion, based at Segontium (Caernarfon) were occasionally active in Llŷn. Indeed, there is evidence that most of the population of the area that were either living in small hill top forts like this one or in lowland hut groups, were 'rounded up' and forced to live in one of three large 'reservation' type communities on top of Garn Fadryn (visible north), Tre'r Ceiri (also visible north) and Garn Boduan.

This rounding up process was the Romans way of exercising military control over the area and took place some time in the first century, A.D. This site has been abandoned since then. As you can see, the Celts of this period were very much concerned in having as great a visibility over the surrounding countryside as possible, this, in order to have early warning of any possible approaches by enemies, either by land or sea. It would have been almost impossible to have assailed them unawares. Looking east-wards there are extensive vistas across Cardigan Bay with the village of Abersoch in the foreground and the mountain peaks of Meirionnydd forming the backdrop. In the right mid-ground can be seen St Tudwals Island East, recently in the news because of its connections with Carla Lane. The old Abersoch life-boat station can be seen on the top of the headland just in front of the Island.

Looking south is a view of Cilan head which forms the eastern horn of Hell's Mouth Bay.

To the north east are the peaks of Snowdonia and then moving northwards to the peak of Yr Eifl (*the fork*) known by tourists as 'The Rivals', (because the 'f' in Welsh is pronounced as 'v', the word 'Yr Eifl' sounds like the English 'rival' this is why they are so called in English, it is not a reference to their relative heights). These peaks are situated on the north coast of Llŷn.

The village of Mynytho sprawls across the near hillside. To the north above Mynytho and situated on top of a rounded hill called Moel Fawr, are the just discernible remains of another windmill.

In 1809 to 1811 a tour was made of the county of Caernarfonshire by a gentleman named Edmund Hyde-Hall. He later published his results in a work entitled imaginatively 'A Description of Caernarvonshire 1809 to 1811'. It can be illuminating for the modern reader to reflect on some of his observations, now that a time span of nearly two hundred years has elapsed. He had this to say, for instance, on the windmill to the north above Mynytho:

'The dismantled remains of a windmill also, the second observed by

me within the County, stands upon Moel Fawr; but with the general supply of water in this part of the country, it is not so much surprising that a mill of this sort should be permitted to go to ruin but that one should ever have been built.'

Moving to the north west can be seen the prominent peak of Garn Fadryn, the plateau of which, supported a large Celtic settlement. On a clear day the sea to the north, which is Caernarfon Bay, is visible. To the west is the huge ridge of Mynydd Rhiw which was the scene of a Neolithic factory producing hand axes and other stone tools which were 'exported' over the whole of Britain, (more about this later).

Off the tip of Mynydd Rhiw appears Ynys Enlli (*Bardsey Island*), and just below Bardsey are the gull islands, Ynys Gwylan-fawr and Ynys Gwylan-fach, which hold large colonies of seabirds.

In front of Mynydd Rhiw is the four mile stretch of Porth Neigwl, a large tract of sand pebbles popular with surfers, sunbathers and walkers.

Llangian village from Pen-y-gaer

The compact village of Llangian is picturesquely presented in front of you, seemingly at your feet. Just in front of this, the meandering stream of Afon Soch cuts through the fertile valley.

Edmund Hyde-Hall had this description of the Afon Soch:

'The various streams or branches of streams by which the parish is traversed are at length collected into the Soch, which forms the boundary line on the side of Llaneingan [sic]. The river is either forded at low water near its mouth, under Abersoch, or is crossed by a bridge of three arches near the church. In any general description of the streams of the county, the Soch has been noticed as remarkable amidst the rapid and transistory swelling of Caernarfon torrents for the winding sluggishness of its motions, and for the continuance of its overflowings. These floods indeed are not only injurious to the adjoining meadows; but occasion the very serious inconvenience of interrupting the communications between the different parts of the adjacent districts.' He says also: *'Upon the main stream itself, or its contributory branches, are worked not less than one fulling, one carding and four cornmills.'*

Greaves and Holland mine under Pen-y-gaer

[3] The exposed rock face on your left is the remains of a quarry, higher up this hill there are some exploratory mine workings that go back into the hill directly under the fort. This took place in 1835 and was a joint venture by John Greaves and Samuel Holland, both these men were major slate mine owners in the Ffestiniog area. They were also prime-movers in the development of the slate shipping trade as well as the subsequent development of Porthmadog harbour: where both Greaves' and Holland's wharfs can be seen. They were mining here for lead and iron ore, the iron was sent to Cardiff. It was not deemed sufficiently remunerative for these two gentlemen and the workings were soon abandoned. The excavation may have taken place to extend the lead mine on Cilan Head.

[4] The house facing you as you enter the village is 'Sgubor Ddegwm'. This is the site of the old village tithe barn. Llangian has had awards for the best kept village in Wales at least once and that was in 1964, plaques commemorating this and others are displayed outside the church hall on a post.

Up until the early part of this century, Llangian boasted its own smithy, which was situated opposite 'Capel Smyrna' which is the nonconformist chapel on your left. This is architecturally, slightly more ornate than is usually seen in this type of building.

The large house on the left with tall red brick chimneys is called Ty'n Llan which means 'Church house'.

Llangian village was the birth place, in 1540, of a famous Welsh bard, Wiliam Owen, known as 'Wiliam Llŷn'.

[5] The church has a noteworthy 15th century roof, the walls of local rubble have been rebuilt and all openings as well as the west bell-cote, are modern. On the south wall may be seen some original footing boulders, dating from the later 13th century. The church was extended in the 15th century when the present roof was constructed and is now unusually long. The roof is of arch-braced and collar beam type and is supported by ten trusses resting on modern wall posts and stone corbels. A nice architectural feature is a cross set in contrasting stone above the porch.

Llangian church

The sandstone font has a date inscription of 1638. There are memorials on the north wall of the chancel to Richard Edwards of Nanhoron, 1704. His sons Thomas Edwards, 1738, and Timothy Edwards, 1749 and his grandson Richard Edwards, 1770, eldest son of the latter. The sculptor was W.T. Hale, of the mid 19th century.

There is another similar memorial on the east wall to Captain Timothy Edwards, Royal Navy, of Nanhoron 1780.

In the church yard to the south is a table-tomb to John Williams of Tyn-y-coed, Dr and Minister 1673 (in Latin). A much more ancient 'doctor' is also buried in this church yard. A few feet to the south west of the church door is a rough stone pillar with three holes visible in the top, this is thought to have been a support for a sundial. On one side of the pillar and barely visible (acid rain has caused rapid recent degeneration) an inscription which reads downwards: 'Meli Medici/Fili Martini/Iacit'. This translates as 'Melus the doctor, son of Martinus he lies (here)'. This stone is of fifth or early sixth century and reflects a continuance of some sort of Roman way of life after the departure of the legions in A.D. 410. This stone is of particular importance in that reference to the professional occupation of laymen are extremely rare. In the Christian inscriptions within Britain, the term 'medicus' does not occur on any other monument.

Inscribed stone in Llangian churchyard

Hyde-Hall had this to say on Llangian church:

'This is a mean building on the left bank of the Soch near the bridge which there connects the parish of Llanengan. Within it is a handsome monument to the memory of Timothy Edwards of Nanhoron, Esquire, father of the present proprietor. He is recorded to have been the captain of the 'Cornwall', a 74 gun ship in 1779, on board of which he was carried off in 1780 by a bilious fever at the age of forty nine, after distinguishing himself in several engagements with the enemy.'

On leaving the church and facing west, there always used to be a ship's figurehead on a cottage near the 'T' junction at the village centre. This was hanging outside but unfortunately, is now in place only in the summer season. If you are here in the summer the profusion of flowers decorating this beautiful village, combined with its secluded pastoral setting, must make it one of the prettiest on the Llŷn Peninsula.

[6] As you reach the main road by the side of 'Land and Sea' and look in that direction, past and behind the houses alongside, you will notice a fairly high raised bank, the seaward end of which is cut through by the present road. This bank is the remains of the outer rampart of an earthwork castle. This was situated on top of the bank and occupied the area where the modern housing estate next to the 'White House Hotel' now stands. This earthwork castle is an example of what is known as a 'motte and bailey' castle. This consisted of a keep or motte on a raised mound, surrounded by the roughly circular area of the bailey also raised like a plateau above the surrounding area which contained other buildings such as kitchens, stables, storehouses etc. The area of the bailey would be surrounded by a wooden palisade. All these buildings, including the keep or motte would have been timber, only later would this timber-keep have been replaced by a stone one.

Castles of this type date from around the middle of the 12th century, a time when Wales was experiencing aggressive incursions from the Normans who had recently conquered England. North West Wales was subject to invasions throughout the 12th century, from the Chester area.

The motte and bailey castle is the classic Norman fortification, often hastily erected in newly conquered areas in an attempt to maintain control over the district. However, it is thought that the native Welsh leaders may have copied this motte and bailey style of fortification in response to the Norman invader, consequently it is not often possible to tell if a site such as 'Castell Abersoch' is a Norman outpost or a native Welsh stronghold.

It is reported that a few 'stone hammers' were found on this site when it was cut through to make the road.

[7] Behind the 'Green', is the life boat station, (re-built in 1994). Adjacent to this and across to the arches are some of the oldest buildings in Abersoch. This is the site of the old boatyard where sailing craft were built. There were 14 vessels constructed here between 1774 and 1854, typical of these were the 'Penrhyn' (a vessel of 76 tons) and the 'New Blessing' (92 tons) both these craft were built in 1811 and were registered in Pwllheli.

[8]This is what Hyde-Hall had to say about Abersoch:

'At Abersoch, consisting of a few houses upon the edge of the St Tudwal's Road, vessels are occasionally built. The timber for which is bought from the opposite coast of Meirionnydd, as the tide flows for some way and some depth up the river, the opportunities for effecting a launch are sufficiently convenient. In the roads are the two islands of St Tudwal, to which the anchorage is indebted for its protection. Upon one of them stands the ruins of a chapel long since disused, and upon them corn was grown in the memory of man, as well as a barn built for its reception. Both of them are now abandoned to the rabbits.

Upon the great headland of Penrhyn Du, which forms the south-east extremity of the county, a lead mine to a considerable extent was explored some years ago, but either from the first expense of working it, or the subsequent inadequacy of the returns, it was soon relinquished, nor has it since been resumed.

Few travellers find their way to this secluded spot, which must indeed, if visited at all, be visited for its own sake; but I can scarcely credit of what I have been assured, that I was the second person of the present generation who had reached it for the purpose of inspection.

Strangers indeed are more frequently seen, but they are in general passengers from vessels detained in the roads who come on here to relieve the tedium of their detention, or in their own words, to stretch their legs.

A good and substantial house such as is called for in order to meet the buffeting of the storm in this bleak region has been built here by the present incumbent, the Rev'd . . . Roberts. But the parsonage is not only a good and substantial house, but a hospitable one; and to its present owner and family for the attendance shown me and the information afforded, I trust I feel that gratitude which this slight testimony of it very inadequately described.'

From the point of view of the history of Abersoch, it is interesting to note how Hyde-Hall describes it as just a few cottages, it demonstrates that the development of the village is owed mainly to the Victorians, as it became a popular holiday resort towards the end of the last century.

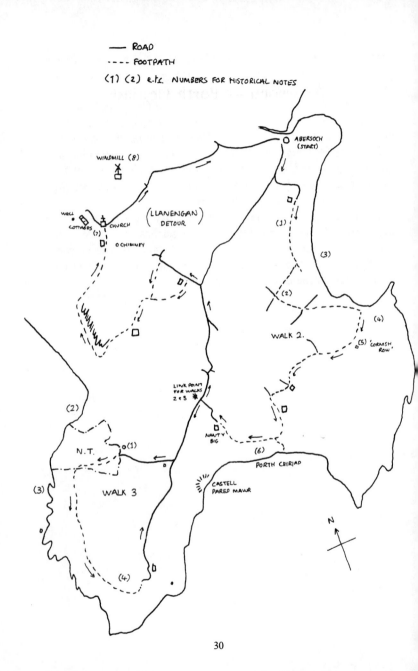

— ROAD

---- FOOTPATH

(1) (2) e.tc. NUMBERS FOR HISTORICAL NOTES

ABERSOCH (START)

WINDMILL (8)

(LLANENGAN) DETOUR

WELL
COTTAGES
CHURCH
(7)
O CHIMNEY

(1)

(3)

(2)

(4)

WALK 2.

(5) 'CORNISH ROW'

LINK POINT FOR WALKS 2 & 3

NANT Y BIG

(2)

N.T.

(1)

(6)

PORTH CEIRIAD

(3)

WALK 3

CASTELL PARED MAWR

(4)

N

Walk 2

Abersoch — Porth Ceiriad

3 hours approximately

Quite a mixture, from lead mines to a sheltered cove on the tip of a headland, if you include the detour it is quite a tiring walk but one you'll always remember.

As before in the Pen-y-gaer walk, *St Tudwals Inn* is as good a place to start as any. Head up the main street for about 150 metres or so and turn left into Lôn Golf. (Follow signs to Golf Club.)

At the large car park make a right turn into the road leading to the golf links and follow the signs for the Golf Course.[1]

When you have reached the club house continue across the links, this track is quite long, about ½ mile.

The road forks to the right near the end of the links, take this fork (at the 12th tee) and continue down the stony track. After a while and a short rise, connect with a tarmacadam surface and turn left.[2]

Abersoch golf links and S.S.S.I.

Follow this footpath until it emerges onto a road, cross this and continue along the path. Keep an eye open here for the birdlife that feeds on the mud flats in front of the old life boat station, several species are represented; Turnstones, Oyster catchers, Redshanks, Dunlins and assorted ducks etc., tide allowing.[3]

At the sharp bend in the lane at the point where you pass a sign on a large gate which indicates 'No Right of Way', turn right up the slope and follow the path, this is very stony and very wet, it is like this in summer and winter alike and after a heavy storm it's more like a river. As you go up this road you will notice on your left the spoil heaps and remains of mine workings.[4]

Continue up the hill and after a 100 metres or so you will see on your left the old pumping station for the mine.[5]

Carry on along this route until you pass an area on your right containing spoil from the mine, this area is private, so best stick to the path.

A little further up the road on the same side you will see some low ruined walling, this area may have been covered by a large storage/sorting house.

As the road swings to the right and becomes a hard surface there is a house on your left, but behind it runs the next section of footpath. Turn onto the garden by the hedge and walk through the large boulders which mark the perimeter of the garden, one of these is pure quartz. Ascend the steps beside the house, the footpath then passes over a stile into a field.

Walk along the field keeping the fence on your right, follow this path around the edge of the fields, admiring the scenery as you go, until you reach a stile — just in front of 'Cim' farmhouse — go over this and walk on, keeping the wall to your left.

On your left, in the garden of the farmhouse is a 19th century well-head pump. Carry on until you reach another stile, this emerges on to a road, cross over this road and in front of you is another stile, this leads over the fields, keep to the right-hand side of the fields.

Continue along this track until you reach another stile — a house just to the right of this field approx. 50 metres is called Crowrach — cross over and go through a gap on your left passing a fallen gate post, head diagonally across the field heading towards the next stile, cross this and continue along the field until you reach yet another stile which leads onto a road. On your right is a cattle grid, but you need to turn left here and walk down the lane, where, in about 50 metres the lane forks, take the right fork and head through the gate towards the caravans in front of you.

The track runs to the left of the caravans. Follow it through the gate down a narrow path.

When you come to the fork, take the left one towards the beach Porth Ceiriad.[6] On reaching the kissing gate which leads onto the beach you will have a choice, if you go down to the beach you will now be on one of the most delightful beaches on the Llŷn peninsula as it is very sheltered and has plenty of good sand, there's usually room for everybody to sit as it is about ½ mile long. Good surfing and fishing, (mainly for skate) or just plain sunbathing.

For those wishing to continue the walk, turn right and follow the track along the cliff edge, do not go through the gate which appears in the fence in a 100 metres or so, but continue up the hill in the direction of the footpath sign, keeping the fence on your left.

At the end of this path and to your left is a gate with a stile, proceed over this and walk past Nant-y-Big farm and on down the road.

At this stage you will have been walking for about 1½ to 2 hours. Keep on this road until it meets up with a larger road, then turn left if you wish to link with the 'Cilan head loop', * (see next section), if not, turn right and follow this road until you reach the crossroads in Sarn Bach. At the crossroads you will see on your left a house which used to be a blacksmiths, next door was a shop. Note the old sign post standing at the crossroads (needs a coat of paint!).

Here a choice of routes is possible, either a simple return to Abersoch along the main road, or for those of you with some remaining energy, an interesting detour overlooking Hell's Mouth Bay, which returns to Abersoch via Llanengan: for this route turn left up the hill towards the Sarn Bach Junior school.

(If the following walk is taken in conjunction with the Abersoch — Porth Ceiriad walks, it will add approximately one hour.)

Turn left and through the gate in front of the school, if this is closed (usually to keep sheep in), use the top entrance which is 150 metres or so further on (Fferm Tŷ Newydd).

Proceed past farm buildings and then, after about 150 metres, arrive at the gate (please close). Take the left path after the gate and proceed down into the valley, turn right at the bottom of the hill in front of a field gate and walk along the path, keeping the rock face on your right. Follow this path over a series of stiles until you reach a farm. Above and on your right you will see the smelting chimney, some 50′ high, go through the gate, and then, just past the farm cottage on the right will be seen the spoil heaps of old mine workings. Zinc was mined in this area as well as lead. Proceed along this path passing the *Sun Inn* on your left, this may be a welcome sight on a warm summers day!

Smelting chimney

Head right when emerging onto the main road, and on your left is the east gate of Llanengan church,[7] opposite the entrance to 'The Rock' restaurant.

On the left side of the road when leaving the village is an old water pump set in a wall with access steps in it, for the benefit of the cottages behind the wall.

The old mill[8] can be seen on your left on top of a hill, as you go up the hill out of the village, it is opposite to a graveyard — the chapel of which has been recently demolished. There is a footpath up to the mill and there are good views to be had from here, so it's well worth the effort.

As you carry on down the hill into Abersoch you will see in front of you a splendid view overlooking St Tudwal's Island East and the Rhinog Mountains.

History notes

[1] Abersoch golf links is an area of common land, comprising 25.3 hectares, it is under joint ownership between Mrs A. Jones, Abersoch, Mrs M. Jones, Abersoch and the Midland Bank Trust Co. Ltd. There are rights to graze 24 cattle and sheep to a grazing density of '8.9 sheep units per hectare'. (Fortunately for the greenkeepers these rights are not exercised: at present anyway!)

The climate of this common land is officially described thus: Bioclimate: Hyperoceanic/slightly cool, moderately moist, exposed. This reference to 'sheep units' applies to other grazing animals as well and the council provide a table of 'conversion coefficients':

    1 beast = 8 sheep
    1 pony/horse = 8 sheep
    1 pig = 5 sheep
    1 goat = 1 sheep
    1 chicken/duck/goose = 0.20 sheep

Within the golf course and to the right of the path you will see an extensive patch of dense low woodland, this is a marsh and fen area and is designated as a nature Conservancy Council Site of Special

Scientific Interest or S.S.S.I. for short. The interest in the area is botanical and ornithological. The old name for this area is 'Cors Lleferin' which means 'trickling marsh'.

[2] Just to the right of this juncture are the remains of old lead mine workings, nothing of particular note remains at this spot. The track you are about to take however, is interesting as it was the bed of the railway track which was used to transport lead ore along to the point where the old life boat station now stands and this is where the ore was loaded aboard ships bound for Pwllheli, and from there to Cardiff & other places for smelting.

[3] The southern shore of the Llŷn peninsula had one great hazard for the Pwllheli shipping trade, Porth Neigwl or to put it more descriptively, Hell's Mouth, this dangerous bay was however, offset by a renowned safe anchorage, namely St Tudwals Roads.

Lewis Morris in his survey of ports and harbours made these remarks in 1748:

> St Tudwals Road (Stidwells):
> This is reckoned to be one of the best roads in Great Britain, it being a good Outlet and so Extensive, that it would contain the whole Royal Navy of England. On the South West Side of this Road there might be made a good dry Harbour, for small Vessels, by running out a Pier of Stones from Penrhyn Du Point to the Northwards.'

Also, in a survey of the creeks & havens of Caernarfonshire made in 1566 St Tudwals was described thus:

> 'Stydwalles, a wyld rode and landyng place where divers shippes do repair without habitacion upon the same and in the Qwenes mai jesties governance.'

An interesting little snippet contemporary with the latter informs us:

> 'Stodewells an Ilande thereunto adjoynyng where is a goodly roade for all shippes at all wynds and verie commodious to come to. It lieth against Wickley in Irelande.'

Geography in Elizabethan times was, sometimes, a rather inexact science!

It was proposed to carry out the construction of a harbour in St Tudwals Roads in 1867, (probably in front of where the old life boat house is now, and inward to where the boat yard stands) as anticipated by Lewis Morris, but it was a pipe-dream and came to nothing.

Although in general, St Tudwals Roads was a safe haven and the south coast of Llŷn was not subject to the same battering from the elements as the northern shore, it still had its fair share of maritime disasters, for instance, in 1818 a foreign ship carrying a cargo of tobacco was wrecked near Abersoch. On October 18th, 1858, a small ship known as a 'flat' and called the 'Ann' was wrecked off St Tudwals (this ship is famous as the one commemorated in the locally well known folk song, 'Flat Hugh Pugh'). She was built in Frodsham, in 1799 and was bought by the master, Captain Hugh Pugh and two friends in 1848. She was smack-rigged, square-sterned, and had a lifting bowsprit. She measured 62' by 15' by 7' and weighed 60 tons. The schooner 'Fossil' was wrecked off Llanbedrog in 1902. In 1904 the schooner 'Gowerian' was wrecked off Abersoch as was another schooner, 'Two Brothers' in 1907. There was a particularly bad storm in March 1903, which brought the steamship 'Telephone' ashore at Abersoch and additionally the ketch 'Seaman' ran aground at Castellmarch, the crew was saved by the lifeboat 'Oldham' of Abersoch.

Undoubtedly the worst maritime tragedy to strike the Abersoch area occurred late in the last century when 16 Porthmadog vessels were weather bound in St Tudwal's Roads, the violence of the storm doomed all but one vessel, the 'Mary Jane', she was saved it is thought, due to the stoutness of her anchor chains.

St Tudwals Roads was also the scene of some considerable piratical activity in former centuries. These various undertakings were firmly linked with the leading gentry at the time, namely the families of Bodfel (nr Pwllheli), Cefnamlwch (nr Tudweiliog) and Castellmarch (nr Abersoch). For example:

In 1536 four ships appears off Ynys Enlli (*Bardsey Island*) two of them were commanded by Captains Thomas Woodfall and John Sergeant, both of dubious reputation. The other two ships had been captured at sea, these carried cargoes of wheat and rye. The four ships came to anchor in St Tudwal's Roads and the captured contraband was soon distributed amongst the inhabitants of the area in any vessel that could be commandeered, or would float. When a commissioner from London was sent to investigate this and similar goings on, it soon emerged that John Griffith of Cefnamlwch and his brother in law, John Wyn ap Hugh of Bodfel, had visited the two captains as they lay at anchor. They tried to explain that as Justices of the Peace they had gone on board because they were suspicious. It emerged, however, that John Wyn had actually bought up most of the cargo of the ships and sold the contents of one of them to John ap Robert of Castellmarch. John Griffith of Cefnamlwch, perhaps because he did not do so well out of the deal, seemed to suffer a fit of 'sour grapes' disguised as righteousness. He describes how 'I John Griffith of Llŷn, esquire, knowing the said John Roberts to have bought pirate goods, took eight men and sailed far out to sea and seized the ship in the Queen's name and the Lord Admiral's and brought it to Porthdinllaen and carried the corn to some guarded place.'

In 1599, at Whitsuntide there arrived in St Tudwal's Roads, a certain captain Hugh Griffith with a French prize in tow. He was the son of Griffith John Griffith of Cefnamlwch, returned after 20 years. There was great merry-making among relatives on shore and aboard. It turns out that this voyage which reached its climax with this homecoming had been financed by Griffith John Griffith of Cefnamlwch. Captain Hugh soon left St Tudwal's Roads, and the day after, one of the Queen's ships arrived there commanded by a Captain Morgan who very much wished to interview Captain Hugh. The reason being that this capture of a French ship was proving a great embarrassment to the English government because they were very much not at war with France. Captain Hugh was warned by the Cefnamlwch family and hastily disappeared. (The above information on pirates comes largely from a paper by Carys Roberts.)

[4] These are the lead mines of Penrhyn Du (black headland) and are of very ancient origin, they are normally associated with 19th century industrial history, but there is evidence of workings here which date from Roman & Phoenician times, indeed, it is said that an anchor stock was found on Porth Ceiriad beach of typical Phoenician design, there is also reputed to be a cliff-cave in the vicinity known as the 'Phoenician cave' which contains human skulls and other bones.

The mines have lead a very sporadic and chequered career since these early times and there is some evidence of probings in mediaeval times.

We enter a period of more certain documentation soon after the Restoration, when development of the mines was undertaken by Lord Herbert of Cherbury — who owned the land — but it was then abandoned for almost 70 years due to transport difficulties and flooding.

A revealing letter written in 1668 by Lord Herbert's agent reports that the 'best works' had been drowned out, but eighty tons of ore have been shipped and sold at £420, and more remains in the store house awaiting the ships' return. The whole of this £420, however, was needed to cover the cost of 18 months of wages for the workers and debts incurred on storage and various provisions for the workmen. This indicates the relatively small scale of the works at that particular time, despite the backing capital of a wealthy landlord.

Next, we hear of some interest and development of the mines in 1734, when the workings and shafts were cleared of water and waste materials. However, when Lewis Morris journeyed in these parts he was able to report in 1748 that all the shafts were extensively flooded and no work was possible.

In 1764, the whole of the mine workings were leased to the mining company, Roe of Macclesfield, who in 1782, introduced a Boulton & Watt steam engine to combat the continuous threat of flooding, his was one of the earliest uses of a steam engine in Caernarfonshire. Nonetheless, despite the initial expense and optimism the output of the mine proved disappointing and Roe transferred his interest to mines near Llanberis in 1785.

We next meet with the entrepreneurial spirit of the Victorians, which likewise inspired a few locals. For instance, in 1870, a local miner, E. Lloyd Roberts, struck a rich ore pocket and sold rights for £5,200, soon after there were eight separate undertakings in the area, employing in the busiest period, around 200 men.

On Jan 1st, 1870 the following article appeared in the Caernarfon & Denbigh Herald:

> ' . . . The old Penrhyn Du mines when first worked gave employment to hundreds of poor people, and it may be stated that in so isolated a portion of the county, the boon was of immense value. For about the last 20 years, however, little has been done at these mines, and the towering chimney stack, and old engine houses almost alone remain to tell the tale of happier and palmier days, but within a few months fresh courage has again been shown at the old place that treasure, the value of which non dare calculate, yet remains. Since midsummer last year (1869) property from sources which a few years ago were considered worthless, has been granted to comparatively poor men, one of whom sold his interest a few months ago (July last), for 6,800,1., and that property is now represented in the Stock Exchange, London . . . at 114,000,1. A discovery has also been made at the 'Assheton' (formerly Old Penrhyn Du Mines) which is valued at 60,000,1., and here it may be remarked is employment for many of our poor. Probably within a few years many such mines will be at work, which will lead to a similar result as that enjoyed by the town of Aberystwyth, where within a radius of 14 miles, the mining interest (lead mines) pays about 120,000,1. a year . . . '

Unfortunately — for some of the investors anyway — the optimism of the article was not fully borne out. Nevertheless, by

1880 'Slaters Directory' recorded three Abersoch based lead mining companies: the East Assheton Mining Co., the Tanybwlch Mining Co., and the West Assheton Mining Co., (Assheton was the name of the owner of the Vaynol estate which held extensive lands in Caernarfonshire. The estate was granted to John Smith the then speaker of the House of Commons. Thomas Assheton succeeded to the estate in 1774, and added the Smith family name to his own).

All this activity was relatively short lived, for most workings had ceased operating by 1895 (most of the information in this section on the lead mines comes from a paper by T.M. Bassett).

[5] Just in front of this and now commemorated by a plaque is 'Cornish Row', these cottages were so called because they were occupied by workers who were brought here from the Cornish tin mines on account of their experience in this kind of work, some of their descendants still live around here.

[6] Although safe for bathers in calm weather, the ship 'Franchise', went aground off Porth Ceiriad in 1855, in thick fog.

The *Franchise* was a large, wooden, full-rigged sailing ship, which was carrying a cargo of cotton and rosin from Charleston to Liverpool and set sail on the 14th January. Letters survive from the Master of the vessel, Captain James Scott, the owners agents in Liverpool Messrs English and Brandon, and the salvage advisors. These letters preserve a vivid and graphic picture of the wrecking of the ship and the subsequent salvage operation:

'We then sounded 33 fathoms and about 10 minutes afterwards the look out, the appearer William Lewis announced he could hear a steamer ahead and the appearer James H. Scott immediately went forward and judging that the sound proceeded from breakers and not from a steamer we braced the yards sharp up and put the helm hard down to haul off the larboard tack. We could not see at this time 20 yards from the vessel. But when the ship came up to wind we made out breakers close under our starboard quarter and the wind soon after falling calm (caused we subsequently found by being under a headland) our vessel was swept by a current towards them. We immediately let go both anchors but before they could bring the ship up she struck heavily. She continued striking heavily and in a short time started several of the butts and we cut away the masts to ease her. The sea now making a fearful breach over her threatening every moment to dash her to pieces, and as the only means of saving our lives not daring to launch the boats in such a sea we fastened a line to a cask. It floated ashore and we were hauled in one by one by the people and all escaped.'

Three local surveyors decided that nothing could be done with her, indeed she was smashed to pieces and cargo was strewn along the length of the beach.

Captain Scott meanwhile, had proceeded to Liverpool to discuss the situation with the owners agent and the consignees of the cargo, he wrote the following letter to the owner on March 12th:

'There has been a meeting of the consignees today to see what was best to be done for the advantage of all parties concerned, I shall proceed to Wales to save all that is possible and sell it to the best advantage. I shall have to cart it over three miles over a very bad road to be reshipped. I expect it will detain me nearly 2 months before I can get clear of everything.'

He further writes:

'In my letter of the 12th I let you understand that the *Franchise* had become a total wreck. She was sold by public sale on the 16th March. There was very little saved from the wreck as it was sanded up so very quick and we were not able to work at it only at low water but I saved a good deal of the metal from the bottom with some of the rigging which I have to dig out of the sand. The proceeds of the sale brought £819. We have saved 2,300 bales of cotton which is now up off the beach in safety but has to be carted 2 miles on a very bad road to be reshipped for Liverpool. We are able to ship about 80 bales per day. I have engaged vessels to carry it to Liverpool at 7 shillings per bale, but it will take a long time to get it all there as the roads are so bad and there is no place to land, only at low water, when the carts will go alongside the vessel, which are all small, there being only 9 feet of water in the harbour at spring tides. I shall remain here and see it all shipped on for Liverpool unless I get instruction to the contrary from you, as I shall not be able to have a settlement till the cargo is in Liverpool. As I wrote you on the 2nd of March and on the 12th March which I hope you received, by the time you receive this I expect to have received instruction from you, how you wish for me to act.'

The shipping of the cotton took until the 23rd April, when Captain Scott was able to quit his lodging in Abersoch. It was the end of his experience of North Wales and of his career with that particular ship-owner.

Llanengan church

[7] Llanengan Church — This church is the finest on the Llŷn peninsula and is well worth a visit. It can be entered by the small lych gate in the road near the pub or through the main entrance in the west tower. The lych gate still incorporates some 16th century timber in its construction.

The foundation of this church is as much legendary as historical. To quote Edmund Hyde-Hall:

'The history of this building, or rather foundation, is like the foundation itself, somewhat antiquated; but as I find it so I tell it.

About the year 616, when Saint Beuno built his church at Clynnog, died King Cadfan, to whom succeeded his son Cadwallon. Contemporary with these personages was Einion Brenin, or Anianus king of the Scots, a considerable prince, it should seem, in that part of the island. Leaving, however, his land and royalty behind him, he came to Llŷn in Gwynedd, where he built a church called in honour of him Llan Eingan Brenin or King Einions' church. He did more, for there too he spent the rest of his days in the fear and service of God. This pious personage was son to Owain Danwyn, the Son of Einion Yrth, son of Cunedda Wledig, king of Cambria and cousin german to the great Maelgwn Gwynedd, king of all Britain.'

In a guide book published in 1940, Eddie Kenrick says:

'Einion was king of Llŷn and as founder of the church, is buried here.'

The church has many features of architectural interest. It consists of a chancel and nave, and a south aisle of the same total length, there is a south porch and an imposing west tower.

The main construction is mostly of the late 15th century and the first third of the 16th century. The west tower was added in 1534, as dated by an inscription.

The church was a popular place of pilgrimage in the later Middle Ages. This earlier church recorded from the 11th century, was probably on the site of the nave on the north west side which was rebuilt late in the 15th century. The chancel at the north east was added c.1520, and the arcade and the south aisle around 1530. Both the chancel and the east end of the south aisle have gable corbels inscribed with apparently 16th century dates, using black letter numerals. The south porch and the double screen and rood loft were probably built at about the same time as the west tower i.e., around 1534.

The church underwent complete restoration in 1847, by the architect Henry Kennedy and further repairs were made in 1938-9.

The roof trusses are mainly of the early 16th century. They are continuous over both aisles: that on the north over the nave and chancel consists of twelve trusses forming eleven bays, that on the south consists of eleven trusses forming ten bays, they all have trch-braced collar beams. Only the roof trusses on the north have wind-braces. It is possible that some of these wind braces belong to the older church roof and may be of the 14th or even 13th century.

The bells of the church are traditionally supposed to have come from the Mediaeval chapel of St Mary on Ynys Enlli (*Bardsey Island*), however, one bears a date of 1624, and the other a date of 1664, which would obviously preclude them from existing in mediaeval times, it is possible that these dates refer to re-casting and not original working, so the tradition cannot be totally discounted.

At the west end of the nave can be seen a large wooden chest known as 'Cyff Engan', it has been dug out of a single baulk of timber, bound with iron straps, the lid is formed of two thick planks also iron-bound, the whole is heavily studded with iron nails, the lid has a slot for the insertion of coins. It should be dated probably around the late-mediaeval but possibly as late as the 17th century.

There is a late 17th century communion table with ball-feet, and the communion rails in the south aisles are also of 17th century date.

The font is of coarse free-stone and of octagonal shape with panelled sides, it is of the 15th or early 16th century.

The beautifully carved screens are framed by heavy sills and head beams, the south screen retains its rood loft, the north screen has been partly reconstructed but due to their similarity of design and execution of workmanship they are probably the work of one man. They probably date from the second quarter of the 16th century. The stalls associated with the screens are of a contemporary date.

Outside on the east between the gables can be seen a rain-water head, dated 1769, and likewise on the west another dated 1757.

Above the main west doorway of the west tower can be seen a long inscription in rustic Roman capitals. The inscription is in two continuous lines which start with the lower, it reads thus:

> I S T V T C A M P A N I C V L V F V I T E D I F I C A T V I
> N H O N O R E S T A E N I A N I R E G I W A L L I A P P
> (upper line) (Tudor pomegranate (L V S S T O T O R A N N
> O D N I M I L I M O (a stalked rose?) C C C C C X X X I I I I I
> H S (three ostrich feathers, Tudor style, followed by a
> *fleur-de-lis* and a defaced emblem).

This is translated as:

> 'Jesus is the light of the whole world, of Aivin, Odin, of myself, of the church and so that his followers shall continue to live for the sake of the future and Eternity, Einion, King of Wales, erected this Church.'

This inscription is in grave danger of total destruction by acid rain.

Not far from the church, just to the side and rear of the small row of cottages to the west of the grave-yard is an ancient holy well. It was believed to possess healing powers. It was cleared out and restored recently. If you walk past the front of the cottages, to the right hand end of the row, access is available to the well, which is reached in 20-30 metres.

There was a locally famous sea captain who was born in Llanengan in 1870, Captain William Roberts. He left school at the age of eleven and worked in the local lead mines for sixpence a day.

A navigation school was flourishing in Llanengan during the last century. It was run by a shoemaker named John Thomas who was described as a fine mathematician by a former pupil of his, John Owen, Bishop of Bangor. Thomas taught navigation to many intending Master Mariners.

[8] The windmill, which is now ruinous, stands about 20' high. It is about 20' in diameter at the base and tapers to about 15' at the top. This was obviously not the top of the original building, indeed there are beam-slots visible for a second floor. The rubble built walls are about 2' thick and would have been externally plastered.

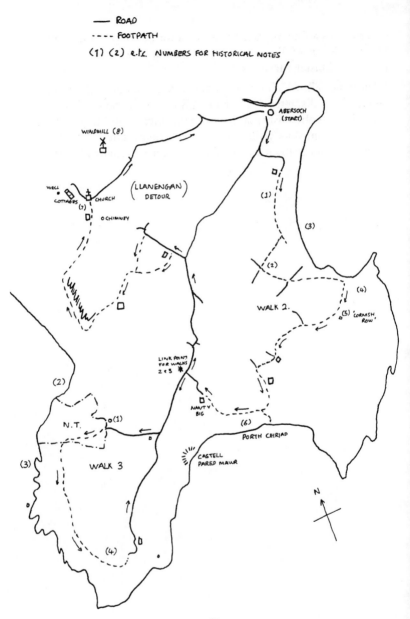

KEY

—— ROAD

---- FOOTPATH

(1) (2) e.t.c. NUMBERS FOR HISTORICAL NOTES

ABERSOCH (START)

WINDMILL (8)

(LLANENGAN) DETOUR

WELL
COTTAGES
CHURCH (7)
CHIMNEY

(1)

(3)

(2)

(4)

WALK 2.

(5) 'CORNISH ROW'

LINK POINT FOR WALKS 2 & 3

(2)

N.T.

NANT Y BIG

(1)

(6)

PORTH CEIRIAD

(3)

WALK 3

CASTELL PARED MAWR

(4)

N

Walk 3

Cilan Head Loop

Approximately 1—1½ hours

The following walk is set on a headland on whose surface Mesolithic Man once wandered. The views from here are some of the best you will see anywhere, especially in the late evening, when, if it is slightly hazy, the whole place takes on a mystical quality. The walk won't tax your energy too much if taken on its own.

Turn left at main road (from ★ in 'Abersoch-Porth Ceiriad' walk) and continue on this road until you reach a right turn at a house called Erw Deg.

A hundred metres or so into the field opposite this turn off will be seen a mound. This is the remains of what is called a promontory fort, this is known as Castell Pared Mawr. It occupies a superb cliff-top position and was sited here, obviously from a defensive standpoint. It is pre-Roman in origin, from the Celtic Iron Age. It is only a small fort and would maybe have accommodated a similar number of people to Pen-y-gaer near Abersoch. It probably ceased to be occupied after the Roman period.

Inland ramparts of Pared Mawr

Proceed down this winding road until you pass over a cattle grid where you will turn left. If you are in a car there is parking on your left.[1]

Look towards Porth Neigwl (*Hell's Mouth Bay*)[2] and walk in that direction, moving over to the walls and boundaries on your left, stick with this track heading due west, until the end of the wall, 200 metres approximately, and then turn left.

View inland from Cilan Head

Just as you reach the end of the wall, and if you wish, turn right and follow the gully to an interesting section of the cliffs at Trwyn y Ffosil (fossil point).[3]

Back on the main path and heading south, keep the field boundaries on your left and the sea on your right.

Keep on this track, passing in a little while a 'trig point' at Pen-y-mynydd. From this point carry on and in a couple of hundred metres you will see a grass-covered promontory on your right called Trwyn Carreg-y-tir (rock-land point), which juts out from the cliffs a little way, from there you will see some magnificent views of the Cilan cliffs.

Rock stratification from Carreg-y-tir

Mine entrance above Carreg-y-tir

When back on your track continue around the headland[4] until in a few hundred metres there is a definite cross track.

Take the left fork and follow this over the ridge in the near distance. You will shortly meet with a fence and a stone step stile, climb over this and head towards what looks like a small open gate with a wooden step set in the ground, go through this and walk towards the farm, you will enter the beginnings of what looks like a funnel caused by two walls of a field coming together into a lane.

You are now coming into a farm called Cilan Uchaf Farm and the track you are now on is *not a footpath* but is a courtesy path, so please take special care here to be as quiet and unobtrusive as possible, go through the green gate and head straight through the farm-yard to connect with the main road again.

Continue along this road back to Abersoch, if you came by car, follow it until you come to the road on the left called the Lôn Las (green lane) with a house on the corner called Erw Deg and walk until you meet the cattle grid and your car, or, keep on the main road until you come to the crossroads at Sarn Bach where you can pick up the short detour through Llanengan, if desired.

History notes

[1] Marked on many editions of the O.S. map is an antiquity called Castell Cilan, it lies just behind the small group of houses on the right as you face Hell's Mouth, it is now thought however, that it is only a natural mound.

[2] Hell's Mouth or Porth Neigwl is a magnificent four mile strand, but it is not called Hell's Mouth without good reason, being one of the most treacherous tracts of coast in the whole of Wales. There have been literally hundreds of vessels which have been lost within its rocky jaws.

Many travel writers over the last couple of centuries who have visited Llŷn have waxed lyrical (or otherwise) about Porth Neigwl (*Hell's Mouth*), let Edmund Hyde-Hall begin:

' . . . and on the west and south Porth Neigwl or Hell's Mouth, magnificently washes its coast. Of the last place, the name and character, infamous for frequent wrecks, have prepared me to contemplate a prospect gloomy, dismal and repulsive. Bare and bleak and exposed to all the storms which rush up the channel it undoubtedly is, but the day on which I first visited and beheld it was lighted up with the finest effulgence of our climate. I ascended from Abersoch, I gained the high ground of the country, and upon the map of the view unrolled before me were traced in the firmest characters both magnificence and beauty. In the fore ground lay a verdant and rich amphitheatre, girdled in on the land side by a succession of hills and slopes, while the sea line was constituted by the noble sweep of the bays selvage. This was its condition of beauty, and if the eye might have been solely trusted, of safety, as it seemed to be protected by the advancing and bold headlands of Penrhyn Du and Rhiw. But in the season of its magnificence and danger the show of protection is fallacious, and while the storm tumbles with full fury into the spreading bay, an indraught into it fails not irretrievably to fix upon the shore the vessel which is once compelled to feel its influence. But how different was that shore as I trod upon its smooth and firm and curving sands that presented only images of amenity and sportfulness upon their surface. This placid scene is again not infrequently deformed and disturbed by the accumulation of vast tumbles of limestone, which as they are thrown up by the violence of the waves, are again swept away by the face of an agency, which amidst its perturbation and confusion has not been traced. Of these masses of stone indeed, a fact very highly curious has been mentioned. Cockles with the fish yet alive are described as being sometimes found in their solidity, and

53

however scepticism may be inclined to deride the assertion, the equivalent facts told respecting blocks of marble and masses of oak, within which living reptiles have been discovered, will induce a pause among those whose belief rests for its regulation upon the extent and quality of the evidence brought forward. If that when duly and patiently scrutinised be not found wanting in any of its required attributes, the wonderful or extraordinary nature of the facts alleged can be no bar to the admission of their existance.'

'Along the shore here are also found in great abundance a hard and black pebble possessing a very fine bite, and capable therefore of very useful application in giving a polish to steel furniture.'

Mr Bingley in his 'North Wales and its Scenery' (1839 edition):

'Few places present so favourable an appearance, and at the same time are so much dreaded by the mariners, as this. It is at the very end of the promontory, and from point to point is supposed to measure about eight miles: it is nearly semicircular. None but strange vessels, even in the most boisterous weather, ever seek for shelter here, for they are soon stranded, and never again return.'

Messrs Baddeley and Ward in the 'Thorough Guide to North Wales' (around 1914):

' . . . the shore of Porth Neigwl or 'Hell's Mouth'. There is nothing in the appearance of the long sandy crescent of this bay to account for the latter name. But for its remoteness, it would be a favourite bathing strand. Such names, however, often have regard to the hidden dangers of the sea, and infrequently a bit of spar standing out of the water suggests their origin. There is another Hell's Mouth on the coast of Anglesey, near Amlwch. 'Hell' (Norse) in the English lakes means 'clear' (Hell Gill, to wit), and in Norway there is a railway station named 'Hell', to which tourists usually take a return ticket.'

The name Porth Neigwl is a reference to one Nigel de Loryng or

Lohareyn, who was granted extensive lands and estates in this area by the Black Prince, including Pwllheli and Nefyn. He had distinguished himself in the wars in Gascony, particularly at the battle of Poitiers.

At the time when Nigel de Loryng was granted lands here there was what is called a 'township' in the Hell's Mouth area, it also took its name from its new owner. The Llŷn had many such townships dotted all over. They must not be thought of in terms of a town as such: simply as a designated area mainly for administrative purposes, and would be a loosely connected community of scattered farmsteads and small holdings. All that remains in evidence of this township is the farm 'Plas Neigwl', this would have been the township centre, and is just inland from the beach.

These townships were of two kinds, 'free' and 'bond'. Free townships were occupied by free peasants who were not tied by work dues etc., to any particular estate owner. Bond Townships were those occupied by 'villeins' who had, in addition to their rents, to perform various specified jobs of work at different times of the year for the lord of the manor. Most free townships contained small groups of bond villeins as well.

When the English government took over Wales with the Edwardian conquest of 1282-3, and people like Nigel de Loryng came to hold power in Welsh lands, it was decided to try and raise more money from the peasantry by commuting some of these time-honoured work dues, into cash payments. This was obviously a heavy burden on the villeins. For example, fourteen villeins at Neigwl were required to work 52 days annually on their Lord's land and to perform duties in connection with the maintenance of the royal hall. No cash rents were collected. After the Conquest this labour-service was changed to a cash payment of a penny a day. This yielded a total of over 3 pounds and became a fixed requirement to be paid by the villeins even if their numbers changed, as it did after the 'Black Death', which reduced their numbers by half, and so the financial burden on each individual was doubled.

The list of wrecks on or around Hell's Mouth, is a doleful one indeed. A quite notable one in the last century involved the schooner *Twelve Apostles*. In 1878, this ship ran aground in bad weather, the crew were saved but the telegram which was sent to the insurers during the event has become part of local folklore, it read '*Twelve Apostles* making water in Hell's Mouth!' after the seriousness of the event had receded somewhat in peoples minds, the unintentional humour of the telegram was fully appreciated.

In 1629, a French ship was lured by false lights from bonfires on the mountain of Rhiw onto the rocks on the northwest end of Hell's Mouth. The vessel was carrying many of the French nobility, who were wearing rich clothing and many jewels. The story goes that the wreckers swarmed aboard as the vessel ran aground killing men and women indiscriminately, cutting off their fingers and ears to obtain the jewels. Two of the wreckers were subsequently hanged.

This whole business of 'wreckers', is not unknown on other parts of the Llŷn coastline, indeed it was, unfortunately, fairly widespread throughout the whole coast of Britain.

When writing an appendix to his book, Hyde-Hall includes the chapter of 'The Recreations and Morals of the Caernarvonshire Folk', he says this on the subject of wrecking:

'One act of wickedness, indeed, which when perpetrated under circumstances of aggravation but too common is perhaps the very worst known in the world, they share with all the inhabitants upon the coasts of our islands. This foul blot upon the national character has here in its practice, it appears, so poisoned the moral sense, that openly and without pretext a pilot has been known to lose the friendly intercourse of his neighbours for warning a stranger vessel of a dangerous situation out of which his experience contributed to extricate her . . . 'I suppose,' says a Welshman to me, 'you Londoners take great credit for not plundering wrecks!'

Here is a quick selection from the long list of maritime dramas which have been played out on this strand:

1824 — an Irish ship wrecked with a cargo of tobacco
1839 — *Transit* with a cargo of cotton
1840 — *Arfestone* with a cargo of gold
1866 — Schooner *Henry Catherine*
1883 — Barque *Penseverenza*
1898 — Schooner *Idea* also schooner *Joseph Nicholson*

[3] Fossil point is so named from the fossil trilobites (Cambrian/Ordovician arthropods) which have been found here, you will also notice some interesting stepped stratification of the cliffs.

[4] The following are some notes on the land-use of this area:

The common land of Cilan Head covers an area of 87.5 hectares in a single unit, there are grazing rights for 900 sheep, 79 cattle, 30 geese and 3 ponies, with a grazing density of 18.8 'sheep units' per hectare.

On Pen Cilan there has been found evidence of very early settlement by Man. Microlith tools (very small stone flakes set together in a piece of wood to form saw-type blades etc) have been found here of a Mesolithic date. These people were hunters and have left no evidence of what their dwellings were like, in fact they might have been largely nomadic in their lifestyle and may have occupied this site only at intervals, probably during the summer. The central area of the headland is always wet, marshy and dotted with small ponds, it may have been the same in Mesolithic times and thus would have been a source of fresh water for dwellers in ancient times, as it has been, until the very recent past.

It is interesting to note that in these times the sea level was much lower than it is now, so that any dwellers on this headland were not, on the south and east at least, living on the sea's edge. From this headland if you look towards Porthmadog, a distance of some 15 miles, to where Sarn Badrig or St Patrick's Causeway juts out into the sea — Sarn Badrig, incidentally, was a danger to shipping perhaps second only in its notoriety to Hell's Mouth. All the bay north of a line roughly from the end of Sarn Badrig across to St Tudwal's Islands and Cilan Head was all dry land. Indeed, there is a legend concerning this Cantre'r Gwaelod (or the lowland hundred).

As recounted in the mediaeval manuscript of the Welsh 'Triads' Seithenyn was the keeper of the sluice gates in the sea wall, he became drunk one night and forgot to close the gates against the incoming tide and the sea covered Cantre'r Gwaelod, all the houses and land contained in it were lost. There were said to be sixteen fortified towns in the land 'superior to all the towns in Wales except Caerleon on the Usk'. Cantre'r Gwaelod was the land held by Gwyddno king of Cardigan. The people who survived the inundation escaped into the lands of Llŷn and Snowdonia.

These legendary events are placed in the 6th or 7th century A.D.

A slight variation of the legend has Seithenyn as a Prince of the country. There is also another variant of the legend which may be older, this speaks of the inundation being caused by a well which could only be stopped from flowing by placing a lid over it. This time Seithenyn the well-keeper is portrayed as a woman, there is a poem on the event in another mediaeval Welsh book the 'Black Book of Carmarthen', it has been translated from the Welsh thus:

> Seithenyn, stand thou forth
> And see the vanguard of the main:
> Gwyddno's plain has it covered.
>
> Accursed be the maiden
> Who let loose after supping,
> Well cup-bearer of the mighty main.
>
> Accursed be the damsel
> Who let it loose after battle,
> Well minister of the high sea.
>
> Mererid's cry from a city's height,
> Even to God is it directed:
> After pride comes a long pause.

Mererid's cry from a city's height today,
Even to God her expiation:
After pride comes reflection.

Mererid's cry o'ercomes me tonight,
Nor can I readily prosper:
After pride comes a fall.

Mererid's cry over strong wines,
Bounteous God has wrought it:
After excess comes privation.

Mererid's cry drives me tonight
From my chamber away:
After insolence comes long death.

Weak-witted Seithenyn's grave is it
Between Kenedyr's Fort and the shore,
With majestic Mor's and Kynran's.

Concerning this section of the Llŷn coastline, there is a captivating description of a voyage in a small local coasting vessel from Aberdaron to Abersoch, which appeared in the Rev. G.J. Freeman's 'Sketches in Wales' written in 1825. The voyage was made at night. After having past the Gull Islands and giving a wide berth to Hell's Mouth! he writes:

> The wind freshened as morning approached, and what with it, and the current, we made here great weigh. I was exceedingly interested in observing the cliffs. They were worn and hollowed by the waves; and the moonlight, that played brilliantly on their moistened surfaces, imparted, by contrast, a yet more fearful blackness and obscurity to the fissures and caverns, in whose labyrinths the surge made a wild and awful music. We were in Ceiriad road when morning dawned . . . we passed Tudwal's islands, and came to anchor about a quarter before three in the morning, at the termination of the cliffs, and in front of the great tract of glistening sand, a mile S. of Abersoch. Our sailors walked with us to that village, where we discharged them.

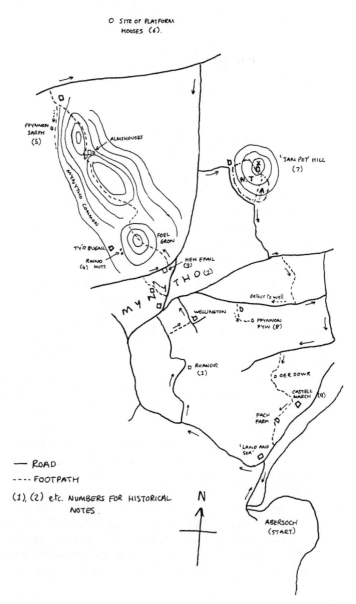

O SITE OF PLATFORM
   HOUSES (6).

FFYNNON
SARPH
(5)

ALMSHOUSES

MYNYTHO COMMON

'JAM POT' HILL
(7)

M T

A

FOEL
GRON

TY'R BUGAIL

RHOS
(4) HUTS

HEN EFAIL
(3)

M Y N Y T H O (2)

DETOUR TO WELL

WELLINGTON

O FFYNNON
FYW (8)

RHANDIR
(1)

O OER DDWR

CASTELL
MARCH (9)

FACH
FARM

'LAND AND
SEA'

—— ROAD

---- FOOTPATH

(1), (2) etc. NUMBERS FOR HISTORICAL
            NOTES.

N

ABERSOCH
(START)

60

Walk 4

Abersoch — Mynytho

4 — 5 hours

This walk is one of those, where although at no stage is it difficult, it can be muddy and at times you will be walking through areas of gorse and heather. It is recommended that you don't wear shorts and do wear boots.

You again will be walking in areas where tourists are seldom seen. Throughout the walk the views are magnificent, pick a sunny day if you can.

As before, the *St Tudwals Inn*, Abersoch, is a good place to begin, this time you're heading down the main road towards the Riverside Hotel.

Follow the road over the bridge and head towards 'Land and Sea', on reaching this, turn left at the hairpin bend and make your way up the hill, being mindful of the traffic here, as there is no pavement, and continue along this road for about ½ mile, after this distance you will pass the Anchorage Inn. When you have reached the brow, a few metres further on than the Inn, you will pass a caravan park on your right and in 50 metres turn right into a road that says 'Private road no tourers'. Keep on this track (this lane leads to Rhandir Farm) to where you will come across a cattle grid with a gap on the right, continue along the path.

After a while you will find yourself in an area where the bustle of life seems so far away, yet you are scarcely off the main road. Garn Fadryn stands like a sentinel in front of you. On your left the sleeping bulk of Mynydd Rhiw lies bathed in sunshine — hopefully — and in front of you the village of Mynytho with its scattered houses clings tightly to the steep hillside as it fills the frame in front of you.

In the field about 50 metres or so to the left of the road is an earth bank called Clawdd Mawr it is up to 18' wide and 6' high and runs between two hedges. It is the remains of an old field boundary. This type of earth bank boundary was common in this area during the 18th century, they were not very efficient as live-stock would climb over them.

At this section you will pass through some very old gate posts and the recumbent remnants of others, the gateways are probably from around the 17th century.

You will shortly be arriving in the farmyard of Rhandir.[1] This farm is probably contemporary with the gateways mentioned earlier, head for the gate to your left and enter.

As you walk on, look right immediately after the gate and over the wall and on a small outbuilding is a dovecote, built on to the existing chimney in brick. This dovecote is quite an unusual feature.

After Rhandir, the road runs through the Llŷn 'Finnish Village' and continues on uphill where you will come to a footpath sign. You are now entering Mynytho.[2] This is where you will turn off.

Since turning on to the footpath, after about 50 metres you will be in an area of rough land where there are many goldfinches.

When you reach the kissing gate, proceed along the path until in a few metres you cross an old stone stile.

Keep on this track until you reach the road where you will turn left, in front of you, and now a private house, is what was the old pub of the village *The Wellington Arms*. Progress on up to a larger road where you will turn left. Walk on for about 200 metres and turn sharp right — almost a hairpin bend, just in front of a chapel.

At the footpath sign in a few dozen metres turn left and walk up to a cottage with a field gate in front of it, go through this, and you will see the path edge around the back of the house, follow this footpath until it emerges on the main road.

When on the main Pwllheli to Aberdaron road, turn right and in 100 metres or so will be seen an old milestone where in about 150 metres at the crown of the bend at a junction, if you look towards St Tudwals' Islands, in the immediate foreground behind a stand of trees is the remains of the old smithy, Hen Efail.[3]

200 metres further on from here you will reach the picnic area at

Mynytho.

If you are in need of a break, this area with its superb vista's over Abersoch and Mynydd Tir-y-cwmwd and their assorted beaches, laid out, as if for inspection, is a place as fine as any.

Behind the picnic area, pick up the path which will take you over the summit of Foel Gron. On reaching the summit, stand at the walkers cairn and face dead north, in front you will see the rocky summit of Garn Saethon (arrow mountain). Next to Garn Saethon and more to the fore-ground is Carneddol. North, north west is Garn Fadryn, and west is the bulk of Mynydd Rhiw.

Looking south is Pen Cilan and the long sandy crescent of Hell's Mouth Bay.

The view east takes in Mynydd Tir-y-cwmwd with the hills of Meirionyddshire in the far background.

Looking north east, there are fine views of Snowdonia and its highest peak, Snowdon.

Y Foel Fawr with mountain backdrop

North, north west is Foel Fawr which you will shortly be climbing, and directly behind that is the highest peak on the Peninsula, 'Yr Eifl' at 564 metres and its adjacent hill Tre'r Ceiri, Garn Fadryn is the second highest at 371 metres.

After absorbing the sights at the summit, head in the direction of Garn Fadryn and make your way down the hillside.

At the bottom you will meet a larger track at which you will turn right and follow for a hundred metres or so until you see a left turn off the path, follow this across the common and pick up a grass track, looking out as you go for the ravens that live here and the odd buzzard which may be gliding overhead.[4]

This track will lead you up to a field where it runs around the field-border to the left. At the end of this field wall where it breaks off into a giant chamfer and opposite the point where you met with the field, you will see on the right behind the wall, the rather miserable remains of the nine alms houses that stood here along with their old field boundaries or allotments. The authors were in conversation with a local gentleman who told us that his mother (now aged 93) used to live in one as a child. It shows how swiftly a dwelling can degenerate once it is no longer occupied.

Here you will take the left branch of the track and head off in the direction of Garn Fadryn.

This path descends through gorse and heather and degrades somewhat as it wends its way towards the farmhouse with the red brick chimneys called Pen Scoits.[5]

If you wish to view the well you may take the pathway to the left as you look towards the wood, with the house on your right, the path goes back along the common, but around the base of it next to the wall. In about 100 metres you will see where the spring rises right next to this wall, under which it flows, and then down through the wood. Upon returning to your route, the path goes around the left side of the building and leads in a couple of hundred metres to a road. As you emerge onto this road there is another ancient site[6] situated a few hundred metres upon the hillside straight in front of you.

Garn Saethon

You will at this point be about 2½ hrs into the walk and approximately half way.

Turn right onto the road and continue up the hill where you will see a farm on your left called Saethon Bach which has an interesting assortment of poultry.

Turn right onto the road at the 'T' junction and continue on for about 500 metres where you will take the next road to your left which will lead past Foel Fawr.

You can if you wish take the path here up to the old windmill —

called in Welsh, Foel Felin Wynt — which is owned by the National Trust. Here, if you're lucky you might see some choughs (rare members of the Crow family, about jackdaw-sized with a long, curved, red beak and red feet). Cross over the stile and proceed up to the windmill, retracing your footsteps on the return.

Proceed on down the road until the 'T' junction with main road, at this junction turn left and then after 20 metres turn right into a footpath which is sign-posted.

In about 50 metres go through a small gate signposted 'footpath', carry on to the next gate and go through. Turn right keeping the hedge on your right and proceed through a series of stiles.

St Tudwals East

At the end of the stiles, enter kissing gate and turn left, this emerges onto a lane in 30 metres where you turn left. There is an ancient well close by.

(At this point, if you wish to visit the well, Ffynnon Fyw — 'well of life' — turn right instead of left and proceed down the lane until a left turn by Capel Horeb. The well is a 100 metres or so down this lane and was believed to have powers for healing the sick, particularly, restoring sight to the blind.)[8]

Return to main route.

Turn right in about 50 metres into the next lane with a 'No Through Road' sign on it.

After 300 metres come to a sharp right bend and follow the road until the end of the actual lane, about 400 metres. About halfway down this lane there is a small group of ancient huts about 100 metres into the marshy fields to the right of the road opposite a large house called Fras.

At the end of the lane you will take the left track with a sign for Oerddwr, which is the name of the cottage down this track and means 'cold water' this is probably a reference to the ford which you will be crossing shortly, 'cold water ford'.

Head down this lane, which is lined either side with Willow trees and accompanied all the time by the sound of a babbling brook, until you reach the field gate with Oerddwr on it, this is usually open. When you are at the cottage, (see bottom of paragraph for wet weather detour) pass around it on the right hand side and then bear left, carry straight on for about 75 metres where you will reach a wet and muddy section — bet you're glad you wore boots! — with a track leading off to the right, but you will be going straight on here and heading up into a field, keeping the field boundary on your right, cross the field into another where you will head diagonally across until you reach a stile which is a wooden fence on top of a stone wall. Cross here and head towards the field gate in front of you.

Detour

(If path beyond cottage is flooded and impassable, retrace your steps back to within 25 metres of the gate with Oerddwr written on it, turn right and cross the green field in front of you heading towards a small stream, cross this on an old door used as a bridge and turn right, continuing until you cross a lane, follow main instructions from here.

From this point if you look across the small valley to your right there is an old cottage called Tŷ Newydd amid some small fields with stone walls, these are some of the remaining original encroachments onto the common during the 18th century. After reaching the gate you will emerge onto a track, turn left heading towards the farm in front of you, this farm is called Muriau. Carry on through the farm yard and through the gate which you will meet in 100 metres. You will now be on a green lane travelling south and in 200 metres go through the next gate — hard to open! but no excuse for not shutting it.

At this juncture it is pleasant to stop for a while and feast your eyes again on the scenery that is in front of you, on your left is Mynydd Tir-y-cwmwd and in front are the St Tudwal's Islands with Pen Benar headland in the foreground and Penrhyn Du jutting out behind that.

Carry on down this track until you reach a point where two paths meet. Take the right and higher path, where below, you will see Castellmarch.[9]

This track will lead you onto a bend which brings you back on yourself where in a few metres you will be heading towards an old ruin, probably a cowshed, pass around the left of this and enter the field gate.

At this point you will think you have gone wrong, as in front of you are several acres of field with no reference points to mark your way, don't worry, we felt like this too, but take your courage in both feet and head diagonally across the field where, after a while, you will see Fach farm and shortly after a stile will appear and you will head for this. This is just before the actual farm. When you have crossed the stile, head towards the small blue garden gate at the end of the second building and before the barn. This will bring you out in the middle of the farm yard with a greenhouse on your right. Take the lane which leads away from the farm until in a few metres you come to a fork, take the right one which is the highest, and follow this until after a 100 metres or so there will be another fork, this time take the left path and carry on to the gate where again if you're anything like us you will struggle to open it.

After passing through this gate you will meet a tarmac path and pass Trefaes Bach on your left, this lane will lead you in a short while to the main road where you will turn right and head back into Abersoch.

History notes

[1] The name Rhandir is a reference to the way in which land, in ancient times, was divided upon inheritance. There is a vital difference in the way in which land and holdings were passed down from one generation to the next in England and Wales. In England, when a landholder with children died, the land which he owned would be inherited by the eldest son, in Wales, the tradition was that on the death of a landowner all holdings were divided equally between all children no matter how numerous they were. This method could obviously reduce a large estate to a collection of smallholdings in only a couple of generations. This meant that the owners of these diminishing lands were always on the lookout for means of acquiring more, by peaceful means or otherwise. The word 'rhandir' was used to denote such 'share-land'.

[2] To visitors who are used to closely compact English villages, somewhere like Mynytho may seem a little strange as it is very much a non-nucleated village, actually, 'village' is perhaps not the correct word and 'settlement' would be better. This spread-out 'no-centre' arrangement would have been even more pronounced before modern developments. The old Mynytho common land, which was subject to an enclosure act in the early 19th century covered an area greater than its present extent. In fact, the structure of the village is the result of illegal encroachment by the

cottagers onto the common land, during the 18th and early 19th centuries, this encroachment was largely forced on the smallholder due to an increase in population around this time, which was more or less nationwide.

These encroachments were accomplished by the traditional method of the 'tŷ unnos' or 'night house'. It was the common belief that if a person could erect a house during the night and have smoke arising from its chimney by dawn, then he would be the legal owner of the cottage and the land around it — as far from his door as he could throw an axe — in one version often quoted. The potential squatter would presumably have prepared the roof-timbers, doors and windows beforehand and would rely on the communal help of friends and neighbours. Thus would appear mushroon-like overnight, new smallholdings across the common land. This sort of thing was going on elsewhere in Llŷn as well, for example, in Rhoshirwaun, Llaniestyn and Rhiw, which also have this spread out appearance.

These early cottages were usually built of mud or clay. Stone was used, often to replace those which were falling down. There are no surviving mud-walled cottages in Mynytho. These mud buildings were basic to the point of disbelief by modern standards and even by the standards of Thomas Pennant, travelling here in the mid 1770's:

> 'The houses of the common people are very mean; made with clay, thatched, and destitute of chimneys.'

The cottages in Mynytho were of three main classes, the 'loftless' cottages built during the 18th century, the 'taflod' or 'croglofft' (half lofted) also of the 18th and early 19th centuries. The third class not of the early period but of the later 19th century, were fully-lofted cottages, many of these latter were still being built in mud.

It may be of some interest to readers to give an idea of the construction methods of these dwellings. The clay walls were up to 2′ thick, they were built in courses on a stone foundation, and were usually between 6′6″ and 9′ in height. They were raised separately and not bound together. The clay used for their construction was found locally as a surface deposit, an area would be cleared of vegetation and watered down if dry, to form a sort of 'pit', chopped straw would be heaped on the clay and then animals would be driven through the pit to mix in the straw and reduce the clay to the right consistency for building. It should be pointed out that clay and earth-walled cottages were only constructed in areas where suitable material was available, in other areas boulders and field clearance stones would be used.

Little is known about the windows of such dwellings, they would have been few and small, some 'tŷ unnos' houses had no windows at all. Bingley in 1804 was able to write:

> 'They (the cottages) are in general so dark, that on first entering, the glare of the light down the chimney alone takes the attention . . . ' (where a chimney existed, that is!)

Also noted by John Evans in 1798:

> 'Some have lattices for the admission of light formed by interwoven sticks: but for the most part light is admitted through the entrance way, for door there is none: but this deficiency is supplied by a hurdle, formed of a few watlings and rushes, which in bad weather is raised perpendicular to stop the gap.'

Wattling was also commonly used for inside partitions within the cottage, they were often daubed over with clay. Many partitions were much less substantial even than wattling. C.F. Innocent, writing on building construction in 1916, was able to note that he had 'been informed by an old Caernarfonshire carpenter that in the Llŷn district, interior partitions used to be made of rushes or straw woven into ropes and twisted in and out of uprights, after the manner of wattlework'. Sometimes the ropes or wattles were spread over with a type of lime plaster, it was traditionally made by mixing a barrowful of white lime with a barrowful of sand and a little water. The mixture was then beaten until it achieved a putty-like consistency.

Partitions in the poorest houses would often be made simply, usually of cloth or even just the use of furniture to divide a cottage into two 'rooms'.

Bingley, in 1812 writes:

> 'Around one table sat the family eating their bread and milk, the usual food of the working class here: from a bucket placed for it in a corner by the daughter, a large fat old sow ate its food: while I ate my bread and butter in the other corner.'

The floor of such cottages would be of mud. Such a floor would be made in the following manner; a few barrowloads of earth, a bucket or two of lime and a barrowful of good quality manure would be mixed and laid and then beaten flat, either with a rammer or the flat of a spade, until 4-5 inches deep. The maker would then have walked and stamped over it in a special pair of flat wooden clogs. Such a floor needed 6-8 weeks to 'set' properly. It could be repaired by wetting and re-smoothing. It was even possible to produce a shine on a mud floor by washing it with sooty water which was often mixed with bullock's blood. Sometimes a hole was made in the floor, and filled with water so that the ducks could be brought in at night to prevent them being stolen!

Sometimes a proper chimney stack was present, more often it was just a hole in the roof. John Evans in 1798 noted that:

> 'An aperture in the roof serves for a chimney. This is not made directly over the fire lest the rain should extinguish it, but a little distance from the perpendicular line. The smoke, therefore, as may be expected, fills the place before it is able to obtain vent.'

An anonymous observer wrote in 1700:

> 'These houses have holes dug in their sides that serve them for a double purpose, both to let in light and to let out smoke. They represent both windows and chimneys.'

Thatching was a common roof covering in Llŷn and persisted well into the 20th century. There were six thatched roofs surviving in Mynytho in the 1920's. The earliest type of roof trusses were of rough poles with bark attached, they were held together by wooden pins. John Evans noted in 1798:

> 'the walls are about six feet high over which are raised maiden poles not even stripped of their bark for rafters, and pegged at top and bottom; a few smaller ones interwoven serve the place of laths; over these are placed heath or rushes, kept down by ropes of the latter, extending net-wise over them.'

With the growth of the slate quarries in the late 18th century, slate gradually became available and was used as a roof covering, initially it was laid and pegged on over an underthatch, it seems they didn't realise that a slate roof on its own was totally waterproof.

In the lowland areas, rushes and reeds were used as thatching materials in addition to the more traditional wheat and straw. The threshed straw stalks were collected in bundles each called a 'tusw', the thatcher would always start on the right-hand gable and would lay strips in horizontal courses about 2′ wide vertically from roof apex to eaves, the courses would overlap by at least half the length of the straw bundles. The thatcher's traditional implement was locally known as a 'pry clustiog'.

The ridge was often turfed or laid with bracken. When completed the roof was roped down by home-made ropes of straw, rush or moorland grasses, they were held in place with hazel or larch pegs, angled upwards to stop water entering.

As stated before, the earliest cottages in the county were the simple single-storied, one-room dwellings. The 'croglofft' or taflod' cottages evolved from these, where one end was covered over to form an upstairs floor, this area would have been occupied by the 'box beds' (gwelyau wenscot). This area under the loft was then called the 'siambar' (from the English 'chamber') and was the parents bedroom as well as the minute kitchen area. The loft or 'taflod' was where any children would sleep: 'The bed was made of boards strewn with straw, in which the hen would sit and lay during the daytime.'

Some of the larger houses would have an annexed 'bwtri' or dairy, whilst the smaller ones would have a small bwtri area in the siamber or a cupboard-bwtri in the main room. Most would have an annexed or totally separate 'beudy' or cowshed. When attached to the house, which was the usual case, it would be on the eastern gable.

Many of these interesting houses survive, at least in part, in Mynytho although most have been modernised, or built over.

Braich is a house only visible from this point by entering the second opening of the 'Finnish village' and walking a few metres where its chimneys can be seen. It was given over by the lessee John Saunders, to his son-in-law Evan Evans, who built a new stone and thatch house on the site. Evan and his wife Margaret are recorded there from 1787 to 1798 in the Faenol estate report around that time but had emigrated to America by 1800. Evan's brother Mark, a sailor, and his wife Ann had another house on the same site also of stone and thatch. They are recorded at Braich in 1786, and died there in 1795.

Hen Efail (its position is described a little later in the walk) was thatched until after 1910, and on a small patch of enclosed land adjoining it, another cottage was built by a subtenant, who held it for 15 shillings per annum plus a weeks work equal to 18 shillings. (The information on vernacular architecture used in the preceding section comes mostly from two papers by Eurwyn William.)

[3] Near the house Hen Efail (old smithy), there used to be a Neolithic burial chamber or cromlech. A cromlech consists usually of three upright stones with a large cap stone placed on top of them to form an open chamber. Unfortunately, nothing now remains of this ancient monument. In 1872 it was noted that the capstone, 12' long and 10' broad, was still intact but the support stones had been broken up and by 1923 only a slight rise in the ground remained to indicate its former position.

[4] If you look down the side of the hill towards the west you will see a small isolated cottage close to the common boundary wall, the cottage is called Tŷ'r Bugail which means 'the shepherd's house' and close to it is the remains of some round huts associated with an enclosure, approximately 25 metres by 18 metres, bounded by a low bank of earth and stone. This site represents a small farming

settlement and possibly there were only two huts at this location. It is almost impossible to date such a settlement accurately as there have been no reliably datable finds associated with any similar hut groups. There are several comparable hut groups all over the Llŷn peninsula in groups of 2-3 or sometimes over 100 (as on the major hill-forts of Tre'r Ceiri, Garn Fadryn and Garn Boduan), and these may have been occupied from pre-Roman times, right through the Roman period and well into the Dark Ages, up to the eve of mediaeval times. As these huts were built in the same way it is impossible to say whether any particular group dates from, say, pre-Roman times or the 6th century A.D.

It is proposed to say a little more on these type of dwellings later in the book when some well preserved exampled will be encountered.

A cairn which was called Carnedd y Brenin Ergan (cairn of King Ergan) used to stand on the south east slope of Mynydd Mynytho but was destroyed for building materials around 1900.

[5] The wood by the side of Pen Scoits is called Gwinllan Sarff which means 'orchard of the serpent'. Close by is a well or spring called Ffynnon Sarff or the 'serpent well' which, if legend is to be believed, is the dwelling place of a large winged serpent — many wells and springs over the whole of Britain have similar legends. This particular well is not as impressive to look at as its legend would suggest, it is simply a spring beside a path, it does not have any associated masonry work as many venerated wells do.

[6] This site is now much ruined. There are the foundations of two platform houses probably of mediaeval date, but nothing remains at present, although a house was shown in a survey of this area in 1816.

[7] We have mentioned this windmill before and noted Edmund Hyde-Hall's comments on it (see walk 'Abersoch-Llangian'). Some of the other names for this hill in addition to Moel Fawr ('big hill') are Moel Felin Wynt ('windmill hill') and Moel Wrgi. In some sources it is stated that the mill was once five storeys high. It is also believed that the mill stands on the course of a vein of copper

which stretched as far as Cilan Head, this is given as a reason for the many times that the windmill has been struck by lightening.

[8] Here is a description of the well as it appeared around the turn of the century:

> 'A *walled Well* (Llangian Parish). — This is situate in an uncultivated area — a *rhos* — just south of the Horeb Congregational Chapel, Mynytho, and bears the name of Ffynnon Fyw ('the live well'). At present it is in a deplorable condition, the walls surrounding the well to within a foot or so of the ground have recently been wantonly thrown down into the interior. Originally these, which enclose an area roughly 8 yards square, were 6 or 7' high. On the west side, near the north corner, was an entrance with a wooden door. Inside the walls was a bath about 4 x 3 yards. Divided from it on the north side, with a narrow walk between, was another small bath or well. Around this was an ambulatory with stone seats against the wall, and steps descending to the water at the two corners of the south side. The spring was just outside the wall on this latter side. That is what the site was like upwards of thirty years ago when the writer first visited the spot, thanks to the late Mr Assheton Smith, of Faenol, who had had the walls repaired and a new door put in. One could wish that another public benefactor came forward to restore this interesting relic of bygone days to its former state. The *rhos* in which the well is situate seems to be a 'common'.

[9] The present house of 'Castellmarch' was built in 1625, at least this is implied by a letter written by Owen Wyn to his father on 25th August, 1625 that states:

> 'Sir William Jones is gone to Castellmarch to lay the foundation stone for the new house.'

This new house seems, from inscriptions within, to have been completed in 1629. Despite internal alterations and modifications the main elevation retains its original form. There is both a fascinating story and a legend associated with Castellmarch; first the legend:

We are here back in the times of King Arthur. One of Arthur's warriors whose name was March Amheirchion, had horses ears. He naturally wished to keep this deformity a secret and so kept his hair and beard long, however, from time to time he needed a bit of a trim, he used a different man each time to trim his hair and beard and when the job was done he would kill them, lest his secret be known. He would then bury them in an area where reeds grew close to the sea. One day a boy was wandering there and cut a reed to make a pipe, when he blew the pipe the sound which came out said 'March Amheirchion has horse's ears'. When this came to the notice of the warrior he threatened to kill the boy, but when he blew the pipe himself it said the same thing. Anyway, March seems to have undergone a softening of the heart, and let the boy off, no longer trying to conceal his ears.

Castellmarch house

The story which follows may be based on true events and is set in the 17th century. The owner of Castellmarch at that time was a certain Sir William Jones who was reputed to be on friendly business terms with a gang of smugglers who were accustomed to run their cargoes ashore under Llanbedrog headland. It appears that Sir William kept his cellar well stocked as a result of these proceedings.

Sir William had in his employ, an extremely over-zealous and strong-minded servant, so much so that the man had actually been dismissed from his service on several occasions but apparently treated the matter as a joke and simply refused to go. Sir William decided that more decisive tactics were required to rid himself of his troublesome domestic. A brilliant idea struck this worthy knight and he held a clandestine meeting with the captain of the smugglers vessel and for a price it was arranged that the gang should come to Castellmarch at night, seize, bind and gag the servant and carry him off to the South of France, or anywhere else for that matter. This operation was carried out without a hitch and Sir William was free to enjoy a peaceful life.

The ensuing cruise of the smuggler vessel was a long one which gave sufficient time for a certain force of character which had asserted itself in the household to show itself on the ocean. Through usefulness, strength of mind, guile, adaptiveness or whatever, this resourceful servant soon became sworn in as a member of the gang and within a year he had risen to be master of the vessel. He decided that a return trip to Abersoch was called for with a spot of revenge to be perpetrated upon the unsuspecting Sir William.

It was decided that Sir William should be entitled to enjoy the same hospitality that had been the lot of his faithful servant over the last couple of years. He was seized and carried off by the same smooth operation as was accomplished on the previous occasion, when dawn approached Sir William found himself gazing back sadly at the fast dwindling coast of Llŷn from the deck of the smuggling vessel, he was once again with the sphere of influence of his old servant, only this time on much worse terms.

Sir William, henceforth, saw a great deal of the world from a mariner's point of view, but after some years the servant decided that he had undergone sufficient punishment and was returned to his old haunts, albeit a changed man.

Llanbedrog

History of Llanbedrog village

Before we start this walk it may be a good idea to give a brief history of the village and its beginnings:

The first evidence of settlement by man in the Llanbedrog area is indicated by the ruined remains of a cromlech on the flank of the headland, (the site of which we will pass in the 'Llanbedrog Headland' walk), it is probably Neolithic in date. This monument is now, sadly, totally destroyed. Other evidence of prehistoric man is indicated by two Iron Age hillforts just to the south west of the village on the Abersoch road — on top of the small hill opposite the Glynllifon Indian Restaurant.

A church was established, possibly on the site of the present building during the Dark Ages, circa 5th-6th centuries, by one Pedrog, who is thought to be originally from Cornwall. His 'church' would have been constructed of mud and wattle with a thatch or turf roof. He would probably have had with him a handful of followers, a small number of whom would have stayed behind at this remote spot to form the nucleus of a religious settlement. As even members of religious settlements need to eat, some land would have been cleared for the growing of crops and some attempt made to domesticate the local wild sheep and goats, one or two mud houses built, and thus slowly, a tiny farming community clung tenaciously to the land below Mynydd Tir y Cwmwd.

By the time of Edward III, three small townships or 'trefi' had developed in the Llanbedrog area, namely Cae Hwsni, Bodwrog and Penyberth. These townships were subordinate to that of Nefyn which had been given its Royal Charter and status as a borough by the Black Prince. The Crown expected payment of royalties for the granting of this distinction and these dues were collected from the surrounding smaller townships, such as those of the Llanbedrog district. Today, Cae Hwsni has disappeared, Bodwrog is a farm on the road to Mynytho and Penyberth is a caravan site at Penrhos. Over the centuries these open townships coalesced into three estates with a central manor house or mansion — the 'plasdy'. The plasdy for the Penyberth estate was at Wern Fawr, a farm on the Rhydyclafdy road. These estate mansions were the homes of the gentry, the peasant population were spread around the area living in mud and wattle huts.

Caernarfonshire as a whole was fairly heavily involved with the proceedings of the Civil War (1642-1649). Cromwell turned his eyes in this direction because western Caernarfonshire was staunchly royalist in its leanings, and the last thing Cromwell wanted was a remote area such as this being in royalist hands. Had this happened, it would have made it a convenient sanctuary for fleeing supporters of Charles I, where they would have been able to regather their strength. Therefore, soldiers of Cromwell's army were sent to try and overrun the houses of the royalist gentry: many of which resided in the Llanbedrog district. Llanbedrog church was used by these soldiers as a stable for their horses, in consequence of which, a large stained glass window was destroyed along with most of the grave yard and stones. Small fragments of this 15th century stained glass window have been replaced and can be seen today, reset in the west window above the gallery.

During the 1740's a pioneering educationalist, Griffith Jones, established schools all over Caernarfonshire in an attempt to combat the almost non-existent system of education prevalent at that time — at least for the peasant classes. These schools operated in the winter months only, as farmwork took precedent over everything else during the summer. In Llanbedrog, this school was held in the tithe barn, currently, the site of the church hall.

Despite the fact that Llanbedrog was such a small, remote and rural community, it could boast of a few local craftsman, namely: a blacksmith, a glass maker, a shoe maker, a fiddle maker and a hatter. These craftsmen would also work on the land and concentrate on their other trades during the slacker farming periods. The village, up until the end of the 18th century, was situated on the seaward side of the present main road. Around this time a group of cottages was constructed in what is now the main part of the village (up the hill from the main road in the direction of Mynytho close to the present *Ship Inn*. This small group of cottages was named 'Pig Street', a name possibly deriving from Pig-y-Llain which means 'point of the meadow', it certainly has nothing to do with pigs! despite a note of Hyde-Hall's which reads: 'It is curious to find this English name established in a part of the Country where so few English people come; while the equivalent term of Mochdre is still preserved in Welsh upon the much frequented road of Conwy.'

There seems to have been a lot of activity in progress along the shoreline of Llanbedrog at this time. Mineral mining had begun on the headland, ships were being built on the beach, and in addition, the shore stretching out from the beach to the headland was a favourite dropping off point for piratical cargoes, usually whiskey, brandy, wines etc.

In 1808 the Madryn family — that of Love Jones Parry — which had been amalgamated with the Wern family at the end of the 18th century, instigated an enclosure act which included the whole of the mountain as well as other areas of the parish. Thus the peasantry was denied its rights of common pasturage on the mountains and headland. This was part of the Great Enclosure Movement.

Despite the drawbacks of enclosure, the village was showing some signs of development and by the mid 1830's there were 25 houses, four taverns, three chapels, a church, a school, two smithies and a flour mill, along with various other assorted craftsmen and traders. Also around this time, some of the more wealthy local farmers invested in the granite mine on the end of the headland at Tir y Cwmwd, but this was not a financial success.

In 1856 the widowed mother of Thomas Love Jones Parry of the Madryn family built Glyn y Weddw Hall (Glyn y Weddw means 'glen of the widow').

At around this period, the construction of the road from Llanbedrog to Pwllheli was begun; approximately along its present course. This tract of land, from about a quarter of a mile north west of Llanbedrog all the way to Pwllheli, was at that time recently reclaimed land. It was a tidal estuary until the cob embankment was built in Pwllheli harbour in 1813, thus preventing the entry of the sea. Previous to this, the road to Pwllheli was sited along a raised spit of land which is visible now as the present shoreline stretching round to Pwllheli: this was still, however, only passable at low water.

Meanwhile, some English reinvestment had taken place at the granite quarry and granite setts were transported by ship to Leeds, Liverpool, Manchester etc., as well as to cities in France; for road making. These setts were loaded onto the ships in the following manner: The schooners would sail as far up the beach as possible at high water and then as the tide receded, farmers, quarrymen and anyone else who could be roped in to help would load carts, barrows, packs on horses etc., and cross the shore to load up the beached vessels before the next high tide arrived, enabling the ships to set sail. By 1908, around three hundred men were employed in the quarries.

In 1896 the Madryn estate was sold. Most of the farms, cottages and smallholdings etc., were bought by their existing tenants — those that could afford to at any rate. In the catalogue of sale, the area was known as 'The Cambrian Riviera'. Glyn y Weddw Hall was bought by an entrepreneurial Cardiff businessman, Solomon Andrews, (who was responsible for considerable development in Pwllheli) he then opened an art gallery in the Hall, where he showed a string of famous exhibits including masterpieces by Turner and Gainsborough. To encourage visitors to this art gallery, Andrews also established a horse drawn carriage service between Llanbedrog and Pwllheli, this emerged in Pwllheli along the present golf links. The terminal in Llanbedrog was where the beach shop now is.

The early 1900's saw the development of Llanbedrog as a tourist resort. A new school was built as well as a new church hall, and the village had its first regular visit by a policeman. This period would seem to have been fairly prosperous for Llanbedrog, with plenty of work for all; new developments taking place and new houses being built. In the light of this it may seem a little strange that it was also a time when many families emigrated to the United States, in search of better living standards. However, this relative prosperity was short lived, for with the onset of the First World War, quarrying virtually ceased and a time of general hardship and depression set in. There was an attempt to alleviate the unemployment problem by the establishment of a 'bombing school' at Penrhos.

Llanbedrog, despite its size, can boast of a few famous Welsh bards. Firstly, in the 18th century was Twm Pedrog who was a local farmer and innkeeper. The next century saw another poet who adopted the bardic name of Pedrog, this was John Owen Williams who was a minister as well as a poet. He spent time as a warehouse man in Liverpool and it was in that city where he aspired to the ministry. He stayed in Liverpool for the rest of his life, but never forgot his Welsh culture and upbringing and continued to write Welsh-language poety. In Welsh literary circles he received the highest accolade on three occasions when he won the chair at the National Eisteddfod. He also reached the pinnacle of Welsh cultural aspirations when he was made the Archdruid of Wales.

In the early 20th century another poetic minister was resident in Llanbedrog, after spending part of his life at Preston and Oxford. This was John Gwenogfryn Evans, who resided at Tremfan Hall and later at Penarwel mansion, both of which he designed himself. He was also a poet and was devoted to printing and editing, an interest he acquired in Australia, where he sailed to despite suffering constant ill health due to persistent typhoid attacks. He became a skillful editor of Welsh books, as well as printing and publishing his own works, together with those of other Welsh authors.

Llanbedrog Church: The church consists basically of a chancel and nave separated by a carved wooden screen, this screen is formed in seven bays and has been re-erected on a modern sill and dates from around the early 16th century. There is evidence on the outside of the church where junctions in the wall indicate that the nave is older than the chancel, but no structural division is visible inside. It is possible that the nave, dates from the 13th century,

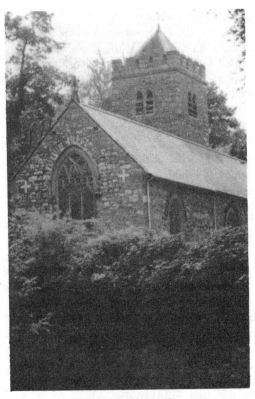

Llanbedrog church

while the chancel dates from the early 16th century, the screen may be contemporary with this latter date.

There is a tablet in the tower which records that the church was repaired in 1827. It was again restored in 1865. The tower containing the porch and belfry was added in 1895. The south doorway and all the windows have been enlarged or renewed.

The belfry contains a bell 12″ x 17″ and inscribed: 1791 LLANBEDROG E: ROBERTS/I: PRICHARD CH: WARDENS.

Inside the church is a large wooden chest 3′9″ x 1′6″ and 2′6″ high, which dates around 1700.

The font is of gritstone and is lead lined, it dates from the late 15th or early 16th century.

There is a memorial tablet inside the church on the east wall of the chancel, to Anne, eldest daughter of Love Parry of Wernfawr 1730. There are further interesting memorials in the church yard in the form of table tombs. Opposite the east wall is the tomb of Mary and Assurance, daughters of Jeffrey Parry, of Rhydolion (in Latin), 1658. Also the tomb of Margaret, wife of Jeffrey Parry, of Rhydolion, 1661, second daughter of Hugh Hughes, of Cefn Llanfair, and Ellen Wynne, heiress of Wernfawr (in Latin). Near the east end of the south wall is the table tomb of Dorothy (Madrin), wife of Rhys Hughes and thenafter, wife of Hugh Bodurda (in Latin) 1671. Lastly, opposite the east wall is the table tomb of Love Parry of Cefn Llanfair 1707.

Inside the church is a silver chalice with the following inscription: *The gift of Love Parry of Cefn, Llanfair Esq to ye parish church of Llanbedrog 1693.*

On the rail of the screen at the north east is a poor box, it is of plain wood construction with two iron straps each with a slot. The lid is inscribed: ARiiAN/Gochion/1774F.

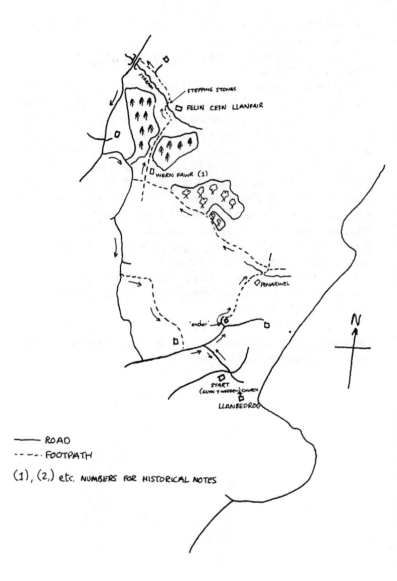

STREAM

STEPPING STONES

☐ FELIN CEFN LLANFAIR

☐ WERN FAWR (1)

☐ PENARWEL

'anchor'

☐

START
(GLYN Y WEDDW) CHURCH

LLANBEDROG

N

———— ROAD
– – – – FOOTPATH

(1), (2,) etc. NUMBERS FOR HISTORICAL NOTES

Walk 5

Llanbedrog — Wern Fawr

2-2½ hours

Start from the car park at the Glyn y Weddw public house, cross the road and walk up the hill opposite the pub, to the first turn on the right, which is Lôn Bribwll. Carry on down this road until you pass the turn off at Glyn y Môr, at this point, you will be looking for the footpath sign on your left. Turn left into this tarmaced lane and on your right you will see a huge anchor. This anchor was salvaged about 15 years ago by its present owner, Griff Ward Jones. It came off the Greek steamer 'Amy' a vessel of some 7,000 tons carrying a cargo of tobacco, that was holed on the dreaded St Patrick's Causeway in 1939. It was lifted from 40' of water, it was only noticed when it got entangled in fishing gear.

Huge Anchor, off the Greek steamer Amy

After crossing the cattle grid, bear right and head towards the gates in front of you. Carry on along this track keeping the wall on your right. After 100 metres you will see a large house with some beautiful roof-top dragon finials: this is Penarwel house.

Penarwel dragons

After a further 100 metres or so, go through an unusual kissing gate and head downhill. At the foot of the hill you will see a stream and a stepping stile in front of you, after crossing these, follow the path bearing right up a medium gradient, when you have reached the top of this, turn left onto the bridle path and proceed along this for a few hundred metres until you reach an open green section, make towards the stone stepping stile by a gate, in front of you, cross this and carry on down the track. If it has been raining or you are walking out of season it will be very wet.

After a short while you will be able to see Foel Fawr on your left, and in the distance in front of you will be Garn Fadryn. The wood on your right in the near distance is called 'Coed Cae Rhos' — this means 'moor field wood'. Follow this lane with its beautiful oaks, and after a fair distance the track will widen and you will come to a junction, * (ref. later) take the right track and the gentle downhill slope into what appears to be a garden, after casting your eyes on the fishpond and the carefully trimmed lawns of the house you will see that it is in fact a garden, so a bit of quiet here, make your way to the rear of the property keeping to the left.[1]

As you come around the rear of the house, a gate will be seen and you head towards this, pass this gate on its right and carry on down the track. After a short while you will see another gate through which you will enter. Proceed along this track with a dense pine wood on your left, called Coed Cefn Llanfair ('the wood of St Mary's church ridge'). Continue along this track with its accompanying babbling brook, and you will, after a short distance see a house, which you pass on the left and then head towards a gate in the corner of the field about 30 metres away — some care should be taken here as the gate swings open away from you, and as you step through, the ground falls away and could deposit the unwary on his or her face.

At the time of writing the next section was extremely wet after some weeks of rain, and one or two slight detours into fields were necessary, but it is not usually this bad in the summer and a new footpath has since been built. You will now be heading towards the ruins of the old mill Felin Cefn Llanfair, visible ahead. The path will take you into a field, keep to the hedge on the left where in a short distance you will come to a stile, cross this and in two metres another one, turn right after these and keeping to the boundary on your right, head towards the path which will become visible

Felin Cefn Llanfair

through the hedge in about 50 metres as a gravel path. This will bring you to a stream.

Keep your eyes peeled here for buzzards and herons as we've nearly always seen them around here.

On crossing the stream on stepping stones, turn left, continue along this track. After some few hundred metres this track will join the road, where you will make a left turn and cross the bridge at Pont Rhyd Beirion.

This next section is mostly on a small unclassified road and is about a mile long.

After climbing the slight gradient you will see Foel Fawr ahead, and to the right of this is the craggy outline of two hills, the first being Carneddol and the second and craggiest is Garn Saethon, which also boasts the remains of an iron age settlement in the shape of a small hill fort. Unfortunately there are no footpaths to this fort.

At a small cross roads at Cefn Llanfair keep straight on.

After a while you will see a footpath on your left, this will shorten the walk and bring you to the point on the route marked earlier with an *, follow this route and retrace your return from the *.

For those who are carrying on, keep on this road until you pass the sign on the left for the 'Llanbedrog Shooting School' at Wern Newydd. About 50 metres up the hill, also on the left, you will see a stile set in the wall, after crossing this, the footpath runs alongside a stone wall, and in a couple of hundred metres arrives at some stone steps in front of another stile, cross this and turn left. Keep along this path with the wall on your right for some distance where you will eventually come across a concrete step-stile set in the wall, cross this and turn left, continue along this path. Head up the slope to the kissing gate at the left end of a wall, enter this gate and follow the track until you meet the main road in a few metres. Turn left at the road and carry on down the hill to the Glyn y Weddw at the bottom.

History notes

[1] This house is called Wern Fawr ('wet area with alder trees') and is of two stories. It is originally of the late 16th or early 17th century but has been much altered over the years. It became the seat of Love Parry the second (1696-1759), who was responsible for the adding of a cross wing. This addition was, however, removed shortly after 1800. There is an added 19th century wing on the south west with a late out-building on the north.

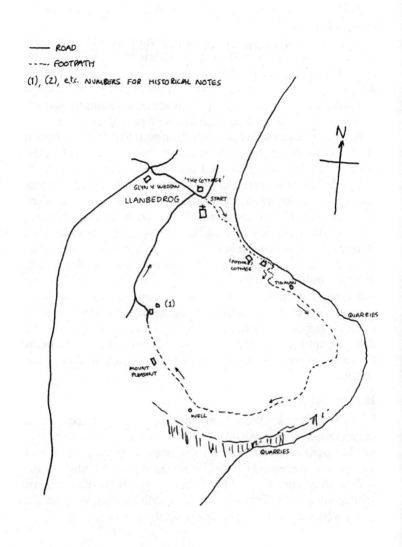

ROAD

------ FOOTPATH

(1), (2), etc. NUMBERS FOR HISTORICAL NOTES

N

GLYN Y WEDDW
'THE COTTAGE'
LLANBEDROG
START
'FOTHR'S
COTTAGE
TINMAN
QUARRIES
(1)
MOUNT
PLEASANT
WELL
QUARRIES

Walk 6

Llanbedrog Headland

1½ hours approximately

The following walk is set on a headland which rises steeply from the beach at Llanbedrog, although the beginning of the walk is quite steep and tiring, the views from the top are quite breathtaking making the plod up the hill well worth the effort.

Start at the Glyn y Weddw public house and take the path to the beach, on reaching this, head across the sands to the far cottage called 'The boathouse', this stands next to an unusual cottage called 'Foxhole', which is faced with Gothic style windows, quite an unusual feature on the Llŷn. This cottage must be one of the most painted and photographed cottages in this area, it dates from the 17th century.

Foxhole cottage

Behind, and to the left of the Boathouse you will see some steps ascending the steep cliff behind the cottages.

If you are here in the spring the first part of the climb will be amongst a carpet of bluebells which grow in profusion here beneath the trees. The way up is quite steep although there are railings for most of the way; for those who suffer badly from a shortage of breath, take your time! The route is quite spectacular, and here and there as you ascend will be seen glimpses through the trees that tantalisingly reveal parts of the vista to come.

Having reached the top the reward for your effort will be spread out before you in the shape of Llanbedrog village lying peacefully beside the sweep of the bay, as it stretches away from you towards Pwllheli, some six miles distant.

The hills forming a backdrop to the village are Carneddol and Mynydd Saethon with Garn Fadryn and Garn Bach beyond them.

Walking on for a few metres will bring you face to face with the 'Tin Man' supposedly representing the ancient Celts, he is a bit the worse for wear now but still something you wouldn't want to bump into in the fog. This is the work of a local artist, Simon Van de Put.

Below you in the village is a fine view of Glyn y Weddw Hall.

Find the path amongst the heather and gorse and follow this along the edge of the hill. Stay on this path until after a while you will again be rewarded with further spectacular views over the St Tudwals Islands and the village of Abersoch.

After some distance along this path you will pass the remains of a well, this was surely of some importance in times past as it has masonry walls surrounding it. Unfortunately we can find no further information on it. Follow the path until it passes a cottage called 'Mount Pleasant' and opposite here is a path to the summit: for those who wish to get to the top, where you can criss-cross the headland. For those that don't, keep to this track until it meets with a larger tarmaced road with a small car park opposite, turn right here and follow this road back into the village of Llanbedrog. Just as you meet some houses, you will see one called Hafdy.[1]

In front of you as you reach the bottom of the hill, just opposite the church hall on the right hand side of the walled garden, is a

Headland well

house called The Cottage. This was built around 1805 and contains cellars of an ancient date. The staircase in the upper part of the house is of c.1725 and is known to have come from the demolished cross wing of Wern Fawr.

History notes

[1] Just off the right hand side of the path near the house called Hafdy ('summer house') is the site of a cromlech, now unfortunately destroyed.

This destruction took place in c.1850. In 1847 it was recorded as Carreg-y-Cromlech. Opposite a field gate next to Hafdy about 30 metres into the gorse and bracken lies what could well have been the capstone. It measures some 8' x 5'.

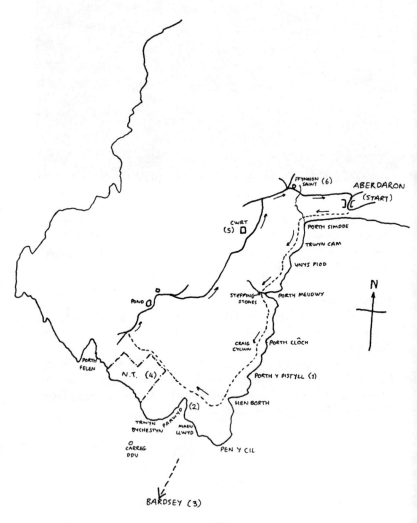

— ROAD

---- FOOTPATH

(1), (2) etc NUMBERS FOR HISTORICAL NOTES

FFYNNON (6) SAINT

ABERDARON (START)

PORTH SIMDDE

TRWYN CAM

CWRT (5)

YNYS PIOD

POND

STEPPING STONES

PORTH MEUDWY

PORTH CLOCH

CRAIG CYLWM

PORTH FELEN

N.T. (4)

PORTH Y PISTYLL (1)

HEN BORTH

(2)

TRWYN BYCHESTYN

PARWYD

MAEN LLWYD

PEN Y CIL

CARREG DDU

N

BARDSEY (3)

Walk 7

Aberdaron — Uwchmynydd

Before setting out for this walk a history of the village of Aberdaron is given. Further information will unfold as the walk proceeds.

Aberdaron with its sandy bay is often referred to as the 'Lands End of Wales'. It is much visited nowadays and indeed seems not to have lacked the occasional traveller in times past. In the 7th century it was the final point of the land route for large numbers of monks fleeing from Bangor Iscoed. Bangor Iscoed, near Wrexham, was one of the greatest monastic houses in Britain. The Saxons attacked and destroyed it completely in 622 A.D., this was such a notable event that it became enshrined in ecclesiastical history and the journey to Ynys Enlli (*Bardsey*) became a recognised pilgrimage for centuries to come. In fact, it was such an arduous journey, from England at least, that in mediaeval times three pilgrimages to Bardsey was regarded as equal to one pilgrimage to Rome. One of their congregation points was in the area of Y Gegin Fawr ('the big kitchen'), whilst waiting for a boat and favourable weather for the final part of their journey, a boat trip to Ynys Enlli (*Bardsey*) and the sanctuary of its monastery. Gegin Fawr is a two storied house of the 17th century.

Aberdaron has also been visited by many writers and travellers over the last couple of centuries and has made various and contrasting impressions, for example, a traveller sometime before the First World War writes:

> 'Aberdaron (principal inn, *The Ship*, very small). This is only a small and not very comely village. There is little English spoken even at the inns . . . The old church of Aberdaron is a heavy, melancholy looking building by the side of the bay. As a place of worship it has been superseded by perhaps a still uglier erection with two towers on the higher ground a little inland.'

Aberdaron village

This contrasts rather interestingly with some observations made by a gentleman from Ireland, who visited not long before the last writer and quoted in 'Blacks' guide to North Wales (1907):

> 'Mr Crockett, whom we find expatiating so far from Galloway, is enthusiastic about the unique features of Aberdaron. "There is no place in the three kingdoms the least like it. It is a village transferred bodily from the operatic stage. The houses are toy like and unconnected . . . Little artificial streams run here and there, dividing the whole place into a series of green islands, as if for the purpose of being crossed by a multiplicity of wooden bridges transported straight from Lilliput".'

High praise indeed! Unfortunately we are back with doom-and-gloom in 'Jenkinsons Practical Guide to North Wales' (1878), in which we are informed:

> 'Aberdaron is a primitive fishing village situated in an

out-of-the-way place 3m. E of the extreme promontory of Llŷn . . . The inn offers only humble accommodation for the tourist.'

Going back a hundred or so years from the latter, Thomas Pennant was inspired to pen the following:

'In a small time I reached Aber-daron, a poor village, at the very end of Caernarfonshire, seated on a sandy bay, beneath some high and sandy cliffs.'

Last but not least, a few words from our old friend Edmund Hyde-Hall who naturally, had a few words to say on the subject:

'Aberdaron . . . Exposed to the full fury of the storm which drives up St George's Channel, it is well fortified for the contest by its lofty and rocky eminences, Mynydd Anhilog and Braich y Pwll (the Langanum Promontorium of ancient geography), Mynydd Mawr, Mynydd Gwyddol and Pen-y-cil Black and horrid, they constitute an iron bound coast except where they are gapped into the small ports of Porthor, Porthorion, Porth Felen and Porth Meudwy . . . Towards the east the parish subsides into a double ravine, down which flow the branches of the Daron and of another small stream. Upon the former of these are not less than five mills, three of which are for grinding corn and two for dressing cloth . . . the parish must be regarded as irretrievably abandoned to the dominion of the blast.'

However, far from being impressed with the actual village of Aberdaron he writes:

'The village of Aberdaron, which lies at the bottom of the bay or roadstead, consists of a few thatched houses, where a small import traffic is carried on of coals and groceries. The exports at present may summarily be described as none.'

So much for the commercial situation of Aberdaron in the early nineteenth century!

As mentioned in the earlier section of the book dealing with Mynytho, the early nineteenth century was a period of population expansion which saw many encroachments of peasant houses onto the various common-lands of Llŷn. Possibly, the principal example of this was in the parish of Aberdaron, on Rhoshirwaun common. Hyde Hall notes:

> ' . . . since the year eighteen hundred, thirty six new houses have been built. Of these the greatest number have been encroachments upon Rhoshirwaun Common, where enclosure has on this account been attended with the usual effect of a contest.'

The Rhoshirwaun enclosure act of 1802, was the first full parliamentary enclosure in Caernarfonshire. Over many years fishermen of Aberdaron had built 'tŷ unnos' type houses on the common and had been permitted to remain there. Under the terms of the act it was proposed to sell their holdings and cottages over their heads, if the encroachments had taken place within the last twenty years. As well as losing their holdings, the peasants were also to lose their fuel-gathering rights on the common. Perhaps not surprisingly the squatters offered forcible resistance and it was thought that the 'opportune arrival of a party of dragoons sent for to England for the purpose', had put an end to resistance, but the act could not be finally put into operation until 1814.

Aberdaron Church:
This church is often known as the 'Cathedral of Llŷn'. It is dedicated to St Hywyn, son of Gwyndaf Hen, of Brittany, who came over with St Cadfan in the 6th century. It was a place of sanctuary to Gruffudd ap Cynan in c.1094 when he escaped from Norman imprisonment in Chester castle. The church canons provided a boat to facilitate his escape to Ireland. It also provided sanctuary for Gruffudd ap Rhys of Deheubarth (a prince of south Wales) against Gruffudd ap Cynan and Henry I in 1115.

The 'Record of Carnarvon' mentions a document dated 1252, which states that the canons of Ynys Enlli (*Bardsey)* had given to the church of Aberdaron sacred vestments with a silver chalice and a missal.

The church consists of a double nave, the northern side is of the 12th century. The magnificent arched doorway is also of the early 12th century. On the outside wall under the belcot, can be seen the remains of a walled up doorway and window. This formerly led to a part of the church which was used as a National School, established in 1835.

During the time of the Restoration (1660), an ancient Holy Water 'stoup' was found in the church yard, it was taken into the church and displayed on a pillar presented for the purpose by Lord Penrhyn.

The font is of the 15th or 16th century, close to it and inset in the wall is a small slate memorial tablet, inscribed 'here layeth the body of Elizabeth Jones, who was buried ye 22d of March 1760, aged 41. Lewis Turbridge died Ag.21.1783.'

In the late fifteenth and early sixteenth centuries the church was extended and enlarged, a southern nave was added together with an arcade of five arches. On one of the pillars can be seen markings which are supposed to have been made by the sharpening of spear or arrow heads. At one time the north wall possessed a low arched doorway which has since been walled up. There are also no windows on this side. At one time the north side of the church possessed a row of mangers, for the feeding of Cromwell's trooper's horses. There are two fine traceried windows in the east wall.

During the war, the altar in the north chancel was presented to the church by Mrs Carreg McCowan of Carreg Plas after it was used for services at a house called 'Pretoria', by a party of Belgian refugees. This Mrs Carreg McCowan has been very generous in her donations to the church, they include: A bible formerly belonging to St Marks church Notting Hill 1863, presented by her, to St Hywyn's in May 1907: a carved wooden plaque for holding wooden collection plates: a carved memorial chair to the memory of Walter John Rhys Carreg, born 1881, died 1911 (he was drowned at Abersoch on Regatta day). This chair, along with the altar rails were carved by John Jones of Brynmawr, Anelog, when the church was restored in 1906: a pulpit in the memory of William Carreg McCowan in 1911. The chancel steps are of Sicilian marble presented by Dr McCowan, husband of Agned Winifed McCowan, niece of Mrs Carreg, and were placed there in June 1905.

On the southern wall can be seen two memorial tablets. One, 'In memory of Herbert Dutton Roberts, who loved to worhip in this ancient church.' He died 28th Feb. 1905, aged 27 and is buried in Smithdown Road cemetery, Liverpool. This memorial is erected by 'one who loved him'. The other, 'In humble thankfulness to Almighty God for much happiness and in most loving memory of Mildred J.E. Bickerton, Christmas Eve 1917 'Blessed are the pure in heart'.

A vestry near the entrance is inscribed: 'In ever affectionate memory of Lieut. Vernon E. Owen 9th (Ser.) Battalion Royal Welch Fusiliers, dearly beloved and only son of the Vicar of Aberdaron, who died of wounds received on active service at Festubert, France, November 29th, 1915, aged 22 years. This vestry was erected by Aberdaron church people and neighbouring friends as a testimony of their deep respect for the first volunteer of the parish during the Great European War.'

The two inscribed stones now to be seen inside the church were originally sited near Capel Anelog, near Aberdaron. They were moved around 1860 to Cefn Amlwch house in order to secure their preservation. The inscriptions date from the early Christian era (5th and 6th centuries) and mark the burial place of two priests. The first inscription names a priest 'Veracius' and reads: VERACIVS/PBR ('presbyter') /HIC/IACIT. The second names 'Senacus' and reads: SENACVS/PRSB ('presbyter') /HIC IACIT/CVM MVLTITV/D(I)NEM/FRATRVM. This translates as 'Senacus lies here with a multitude of brethren'. It may suggest that here is a grave within the cemetery of an ecclesiastical settlement, which may have formed the nucleus of the later 'clas' church at Aberdaron. (a clas church is a 'mother' church.)

The church had fallen into extreme disrepair by 1841, when a second church was built outside the village to replace it, this was not used, however, as the old church was restored in 1846.

The graveyard is reputed to be the largest in the Llŷn and at one time some graves were in danger of being exposed by the action of the sea. There is a gravestone dating from 1787, it is the grave of the last person to be hanged in Llŷn for sheep stealing. It bears the inscription 'Tu ne deroberas point'.

There is an interesting grave of an old sea captain with the following verse inscription:

> The roaring wind and raging seas
> Have tossed me to and fro,
> In spite of both, by God's decree
> I harbour here below,
> When safe at anchor I do lay
> With many of our fleet,
> Yet once again, I must set sail
> Our saviour Christ to meet.

Probably the most famous 'product' of Aberdaron has been in the person of Richard Jones, better known as 'Dic Aberdaron'. Dic was a strange phenomenon, the descendant of generations of peasants who could probably not even read or write, Dic acquired mastery of 13 or 14 languages, some say as many as 35. He was born in 1780, at a house between Aberdaron and Porthoer (*Whistling Sands*) and was the son of a carpenter, but it was not from him that he acquired his craving for strange tongues. His father, who was also a part-time fisherman, was obviously keen that Dic should be, like himself, either a carpenter or fisherman. All Dic wanted to do was read books and learn languages, this naturally lead to much domestic friction, 'If detected with a book he was assuredly beaten, so that to use his own expression, almost all the bread that he ate was "steeped in tears".' It is then even more remarkable that with this singular lack of encouragement, Dic proceeded to the linguistic heights that he did.

Dic had no formal schooling but was often to be seen hanging around the schoolroom, and there, using books he found lying around, started his linguistic career by learning to read Welsh, and soon afterward by the same laborious method he learned English.

By the age of 20, tired of being cursed and beaten by his father for failing to become a proficient carpenter or fisherman, Dic took to wandering. He got as far as Liverpool, via Caernarfon and Bangor. By this time his stock of languages was increasing noticeably, he had learned Latin, Greek and Hebrew. He acquired Italian and German through association with travellers and peddlers of those nationalities, likewise French, Russian and Scandinavian.

Dic would often find patrons to aid his studies, bishops, clergymen and traders would often give him work in garden, field or stable, and he would choose as payment any books on languages or grammar with which they might care to part. One patron was heard to ask, when observing him to discard the fork with which he had been pitching hay and go to his pocket for a volume, 'What book is that?' 'Ethiopic Grammar!' was the short reply, and to it without further comment or observation, Dic applied, until satisfied for the time with his studies, he then rose and resumed his work with the fork.

Dic's personal appearance was every bit as bizarre as his mental processes. Paintings of him which survive show a face and head covered with bushy black hair, from the depths of which peer two bright beady eyes. His dress was individual in the extreme, as his precious library was carried at all times upon his person, concealed in a multitude of pockets which gave him an inflated, abnormal appearance. He would often be seen in a coloured huntsmans jacket, patched and covered with countless pockets, his ragged, patched and bepocketed trousers were several sizes too large and rolled up at the bottom, his feet encased in objects barely recognisable as boots, and a battered silk, vaguely hat-like encumbrance on his head.

Peering out from amongst his matted shoulder-length hair would usually be seen his favourite companion, a much loved cat. Around his neck was slung a French horn which he acquired in Caernarfon from a French deserter, and on this at inopportune and inappropriate moments, he would give horrendous blasts and proceed to deliver odes in foreign languages in a stentorian voice, much to the dismay and alarm of surrounding animals, birds and peasantry. Dic at one time must have felt that his dress lacked a little something, and so to lift it slightly above the realms of the ordinary he adopted a cast-off blue and silver cavalry jacket, jauntingly offset by a cap made from the head of a hare with the ears wired so they stuck up in the air. As a finishing touch to this head-gear, he hung from its ears several long strips of cloth on which were inscribed, no doubt, profound sentences in Greek and Hebrew, and in this attire, complete with cat, books and horn, he would drone out the 'Song of Moses' in fluent Hebrew to astonished Welsh villagers.

Dic was famous throughout the whole of North Wales, but he was also a well known figure much further afield, as far as London and Dover.

Dic was also accounted in his latter days as something of a magician and cabalist with the ability to call up the devil. Indeed he used to supplement his meagre earnings as a labourer by telling fortunes.

He resided for a time in Denbighshire and in 1843 at the age of 63, he was suddenly taken ill and died, being buried in the church yard of St Asaph, where his grave is to be seen today.

Dic is now a figure of folk-lore in Llŷn as are some of the tales about him, such as his near shipwreck at Llanaelhaearn, his strangely constructed grandfather clock, and the time he once advised a man to cross a swollen river by riding on a calf, both, rather unsurprisingly, were drowned.

> St Hywyn's Church lies sleeping
> With its Ffynnon Fair so clear,
> Long years have fled in weeping
> Those sons that were so dear
> Ne'er produced a son so lowly,
> With lingual traits so deep,
> As wild Dic of Aberdaron,
> Whose memory old peasants keep.

Richard Robert Jones, may he long be remembered.

On the subject of folk-lore there are some interesting snippets from the Aberdaron area concerning fairies or the little people or

'*Tylwyth Teg*', as they are known in Welsh. In his large book entitled 'Celtic Folklore' published in 1901, John Rhys writes:

'During my visit to Aberdaron, my wife and I went to the top of Mynydd Anelog, and on the way up we passed a cottage, where a very illiterate woman told us that the *Tylwyth Teg* formerly frequented the mountain when there was mist on it; that they changed people's children if they were left alone on the ground; and that the way to get the right child back was to leave the fairy urchin without being touched or fed. She also said that, after baking, people left the *gradell* (a gradell was a flat round iron like a griddle or an Irish skillet on which loaves were baked) for the fairies to do their baking: they would then leave a cake behind them as payment. As for the fairies just now, they have been exorcised (wedi'i ffrymu) for some length of time.

Mrs Williams of Pwll Defaid, told me that the rock opposite, called Clip y Gylfinir, or Bodwyddog mountain, a part of Mynydd y Rhiw, was the result of the *Tylwyth Teg* and that they revelled there when it was covered with mist; she added that a neighbouring farm called Bodermud Isa, was well known at one time as a place where the fairies came to do their baking. But the most remarkable tale I had in the neighbourhood of Aberdaron was from Evan Williams, a smith who lives at Yr Ardd Las, on Rhos Hirwaen. If I remember rightly, he is a native of Llaniestyn, and what he told me relates to a farmer's wife who lived at the Nant in that parish. Now this old lady was frequently visited by a fairy who used to borrow a *gradell* from her. This she used to get, and she returned it with a loaf borne on her head in acknowledgement. But one day she came to ask for the loan of a *troell bach* or wheel for spinning flax. When handing her this, the farmer's wife wished to know her name, as she came so often, but she refused to tell her. However she watched her spinning, and overheard her singing to the whirr of the wheel:

'Bychan a wydda' hi
Mai Sili go Dwt
Yw f'enw i.'

'Little did she know
That Sili go Dwt
Is my name.'

The smith told me another short tale, about a farmer who lived not long ago at Deunant, close to Aberdaron. The latter used, as is the wont of country people, to go out a few steps in front of his house every night to . . . ! before going to bed; but once upon a time, while he was standing there, a stranger stood by him and spoke to him saying that he had not any idea how he and his family were annoyed by him. The farmer asked how that could be, to which the stranger replied that his house was just below where they stood, and if he would only stand on his foot he would see that what he said was true. The farmer complying, put his foot on the others' foot, and then he could clearly see that all the slops from his house went down the chimney of the other's house, which stood far below in a street he had never seen before. The fairy then advised him to have his door in the other side of his house, and that if he did so his cattle would never suffer from the *clwy'byr* ('short disease' or possibly anthrax). The result was that the farmer obeyed, and had his door walled up and another made on the other side of the house: ever after he was a most prosperous man, and nobody was so successful as he in rearing stock in all that part of the country. To place the whole thing beyond the possibility of doubt, Evan Williams assured me that he had often seen the farmer's house with the front door in the back.'

Aberdaron bay, and in particular Bardsey Sound are notorious like Porth Neigwl (*Hell's Mouth*), as a danger to shipping. The tide-race in the sound when a spring tide is flooding, is reputed to be the seventh fastest in the world, and with a wind against such a tide it can readily be appreciated what a treacherous stretch of water Swnt Enlli (*Bardsey Sound*) is. Here follows a few examples of some shipwrecks of Aberdaron and the Sound:

1836 — Sailing ship *Rhine* sunk in Bardsey Sound

1849 — Schooner *Mermaid* sunk in Bardsey Sound

1858 — Small ship sunk in Bardsey Sound

1864 — Schooner *Racer* of Pwllheli lost in Bardsey Sound

1865 — Sailing ship *Austria* lost near Rhiw

1868 — A ship with a cargo of wood lost at Aberdaron

1869 — Schooner *Voelas* lost in Bardsey Sound. (In 1878 a fog horn was installed on Bardsey)

1914 — Schooner *Harvest Home* wrecked near Uwchmyndd with a cargo of china clay

1918 — Ship *Oransa* wrecked on Bardsey

1934 — SS *Pultney* lost off Bardsey after a collision with SS 'Thelma'

In addition to these historical shipwrecks, there is a legendary one. The legend has it that King Arthur's ship Caswennan was wrecked in Bardsey Sound. The story is remembered in a traditional name for Bardsey strait of Ffrydiau Caswennan, and some rocks on the shore of Bardsey are called Creigiau Caswennan.

The Walk — Time: 4-5 hours

This is a clifftop walk which shouldn't be missed as the scenery is quite spectacular, and if you are lucky enough to have a bright but blustery day you will be rewarded with memories of rugged coastlines and heaving seas all set against a backdrop of islands.

The walk starts at the car park in Aberdaron, where you may leave your car, set out onto the main road and turn left and immediate left again, beginning the climb up the hill above the car park. This road will lead you to the first footpath sign, at which, you turn into the path and proceed past the house called Gwynfa where the path crosses a small wooden bridge over the Afon Saint, in a few metres stop and take the short path on your left which overlooks the waterfall.

Retrace your steps to the main path and continue, taking in the views of the beach as you go.

This corner of the beach is called Porth y Simdde, ('port of the chimney'). Remains can be seen of an old building at the mouth of the river Saint. This was probably a corn grinding mill. Remains can also be seen of an old jetty running into the sea.

In a couple of hundred metres or so you will notice a small promontory in the cliff this is called Trwyn Cam.

At the fork in the path take the top one as the other goes down to the beach, continue along this path until after a while you will pass through a kissing gate, if at this point you look towards the sea you will notice a large detached rock, this is called Ynys Piod ('magpie island'). The path leads on to Porth Meudwy, ('port of the hermit').

Porth Meudwy

Port Meudwy, a small fishing port, was an embarkation point for the pilgrims wishing to go to Ynys Enlli (*Bardsey*). It still has a timeless quality about it as you shuffle between the lobster pots and fishing boats to get to the small stream opposite the path you have just descended. Cross the stream and make your way up the steep slope in front of you and over the stile (at this point you can cut off from the path and take the other signposted track back to the road).

Carry along this path in the direction of Porth Cloch ('port of the bell') where you will take the new and slightly higher path: the old path which was much the more exciting one, is unfortunately now somewhat dangerous.

Keep to this track and cross over Craig Cwlwm '(knotty crag'), and into the small quarry, which was worked, possibly in the last century. (Again, at this juncture there is a path to the Aberdaron road.)

Head along this path passing Porth y Pistyll ('port of the waterspout').[1]

In a while you will come to Hen Borth ('old port'), where you will bear left on the path from the wire fence and head towards a small broken wall, about 75 metres, follow this up the steep slope towards the National Trust sign at the top of the hill. On joining this path, turn left on to it until it heads into some small crags and peters out. At this point you will be further repaid for all this walking by superb vista's across Bardsey Sound to the island itself, where, depending on the weather, it will be showing one of its many moods.[3]

In the foreground is the attendant small island of Carreg Ddu ('black rock'), a barren rock, and a resting place for seals and sea-birds. Beyond this, in the distance, is the barely discernible rocks of Maen Bugail ('shepherd's stone'). Directly in front of you is the cove of Parwyd.[2]

After you have taken in the atmosphere of this very special place, head upwards towards the stone 'walkers' cairn at the summit of Pen y Cil (headland in the corner) where you will take the safe route to the National Trust property of Bychestyn.[4]

Head towards the stile inland, and cross this, heading left to the gates and through onto the headland.

Walk along this path in a westerly direction (sea on the left) heading towards Mynydd Mawr, until you are confronted by a fence, at this, turn right and walk along until you reach the end of the fence where you will take the left track through the gate. Head along this lane until in a short distance it meets with another slightly broader track where you will bear right. Continue along this lane until you reach a pond Pwll Cyw, ('chicken pond'!) where the path splits left and right (the left path takes you up onto Mynydd Mawr). Take the path to your right and follow this small road to the farm called Cwrt, which is about half a mile distant.[5]

After passing this farm, the second gate on your right is the entrance to Bryn Crocbren ('gallows hill').

Keep on this road until you meet with a 'T' junction where you will turn right and in a little while come to another 'T' junction where you will turn right again, bringing you onto the main road where you will shortly meet up with your car. At the last 'T' junction will be found Ffynnon Saint, ('the saint's well').[6] The overgrown and barely visible well is positioned opposite the house of the National Trust warden about 10 metres into some undergrowth and is in a deplorable condition.

History notes

[1] At Porth y Pistyll was discovered what is known as an 'industry of flint and stone', it was a location where Man in the Neolithic period prepared tools for use in everyday life such as knives, scrapers, axes, arrowheads, fish-hooks etc. One particular find of the Neolithic or early Bronze Age period is a 'double ended hammer-stone' which measures 4½″ x 1½-2″ diameter.

[2] The large cove in front of you is called Parwyd, which means 'partition'. At Parwyd in May 1959 and again in the April of 1961, on the top of the cliff which rises from the sea, were found five stone blades. Three of these blades were comparatively short, being between 2¼″ and 3¼″ long and between 1″ and 1¼″ wide. The remaining two are larger being somewhere between 5 and 5¾″ long with a width of between 1 and 1¼″, the greatest thickness of any of the blades is just over ½″. Two of these blades show

evidence of having been used as awls. The main interest in these tools lies in the fine quality of their construction.

[3] Bardsey:

> 'To Bardsey was the lord of ocean bound;
> Bardsey, the holy islet in whose soil
> Did many a Chief and many a Saint repose
> His great progenitors. He mounts the skiff;
> Her canvas swells before the breeze, the sea
> Sings round her sparkling keel, and soon the Lord
> Of Ocean (Madoc) treads the venerable shore.'

Southey's Madoc

Ynys Enlli, known by the English as Bardsey, has also been called 'The Rome of Britain' and 'The Iona of Wales'. Bardsey is a Viking name and means either, Island of the Bard's or Bard's Island — referring to an individual named 'Bard'. There are also a couple of choices when it comes to the meaning of the Welsh name as it may mean 'Isle of the Currents' (for obvious reasons) or it may be a reference to one Benlli Gawr ('Benlli the giant') who is said to have been king of Powys and who was deposed by Germanus (Garmon) in 447 A.D.

The origins of religious settlement on Bardsey go back deep into the Dark Ages. It was certainly established as a refuge by 622 A.D. when the monks of Bangor Iscoed fled there to escape the Saxons. There may have been monks' cells on the island for at least a couple of centuries before this date. St Cadfan is the Saint usually associated with the first religious foundation on Bardsey. Cadfan, with a large company of other 'saints' arrived in Britain from Brittany around 516 A.D. having been driven from his former territories by the Franks. Some of these other 'saints' established churches all over North Wales and include the well known Padarn as well as Gwyndaf and Hywyn (who established the church in Aberdaron). Over the centuries this monastic settlement became one of noted importance — the well known legend of the 20,000 buried saints is a testimony to this importance in the eyes of the world, even if the figure is not literally correct it shows the measure

112

of importance with which the island was held.

This remote religious sanctuary, before the Norman conquest, was constructed on very simple lines. The monks lived in separate 'cells' or huts which would have been wattle or stone built; there would have been a small church, a hospice and a cell for the Abbot, these were later built of timber and wattle. The whole was then enclosed by a wall, this arrangement was called a 'llan'. It is almost impossible for us today to comprehend the awesome simplicity and austerity of the life led by these monks in this remote, gale-swept, bleak and treeless island; they must have indeed felt that they were dwelling on the edge of the world.

Cadfan, then, was the first Abbot, he was succeeded by Lleuddad (Laudatus) whose name is preserved in the area, as in Gerddi Lleuddad ('Lleuddad's gardens') on Bardsey, Ogof Lleuddad ('Lleuddad's cave') near Aberdaron and Ffynnon Lleuddad ('Lleuddad's well') in the parish of Bryncroes.

There is a legend connected with this Lleuddad, or Laudatus, let the author of 'North Wales and its Scenery' (1798), the Rev. Bingley tell the story:

'There is an old legend yet extant, written in monkish Latin, which assures us that the Almighty had entered into a particular covenent with Laudatus, the first abbot of Bardsey, in return for the piety of his monks. By this the peculiar privilege of dying according to seniority, the oldest always going off first, was assured to all the religious of the monastery of Bardsey. By this privilege it is stated, that everyone knew very nearly the time of his own departure. The following is a translation of it: "At the original foundation of the monastery of this island, the Lord God, who attendeth to the petitions of the just, at the earnest request of the holy Laudatus, the first abbot, entered into a covenant with that holy man, and miraculously confirmed his promise unto him and his successors, the abbots and monks, forever, while they should continue to lead holy and religious lives, that they should die by succession, that is, the oldest should go first, like a shock of corn ripe for the sickle.

Being thus warned of the approach of death, each of them, therefore, should watch, as not knowing at what exact hour the thief might come: and being thus always prepared, each of them, by turns, should lay aside his earthly body. God, who is ever faithful, kept this covenant, as he formely did with the Israelites, inviolate, until the monks no longer led a religious life, but began to profane and defile God's sanctuary by their fornications and abominable crimes.

Wherefore, after this, they were permitted to die like other men, sometimes the older, sometimes the younger, and sometimes the middle aged first; and being thus uncertain of the approach of death, they were compelled to submit to the general laws of mortality. Thus, when they ceased to lead a wholly and religious life, God's miraculous covenant also ceased: And do thou therefore, O God, have mercy upon us".'

Saint Dubricus (Dyfrig) is said to have retired to Bardsey and to have died there around 522 A.D. — His relics were transferred to Llandaf and installed there with great ceremony in 1120, by Bishop Urban. Other well known saints who are said to be buried there are David, Deiniol and Beuno. The 12th century bard Meilir hoped to end his days on Bardsey:

'A place that is solitary
By wayfarers untrodden
Around its graveyard heaves
The bosom of the deep
The fair island of Mary,
The Holy isle of Saints.'

The Abbey was dedicated to the Blessed Virgin Mary. The foundations of a similarly dedicated chapel are still to be seen on the mainland in association with a well of the same name. This dedication is probably to be dated after the establishment of the Augustinian Canons, or Black Canons (from the colour of their habit) on Bardsey soon after 1100 A.D. Certain privileges were granted to the Canons of Bardsey such as freedom from toll on the sale of cattle — they held extensive farmlands on the mainland as well as the island itself — and 'rights to wreckage' of the sea on the whole of the coast including the mainland coast around Aberdaron, these privileges contributed to some ill feeling between the Canons of Bardsey and the secular Canons of Aberdaron. There is a document of 1252, concerning the two parties and is an agreement settling various controversies between them.

As has been stated before, Bardsey had always figured prominently as a place of pilgrimage. The pilgrim would have arrived in Llŷn from one of two directions:

The journey from the north, would be approached via Bangor, and having visited the Cathedral, he would make his way through the walled town of Caernarfon to Clynnog Fawr and the ancient church of St Beuno. He would then cross Yr Eifl and walk on through Pistyll towards Nefyn, and along the shore to Llangwnnadl and finally to Aberdaron.

If his journey brought him from the south, he would come through Pwllheli, arriving there perhaps by ship, and then on towards Llanengan via the church there. Then, on past Hell's Mouth and the climb towards Rhiw and on in the direction of the church of St Hywyn on the shore at Aberdaron.

Here and there on the journey, he would practice his devotions in a number of the old churches of Llŷn, spending nights at certain recognised lodgings where he could count on a meal and a bed, warming himself in front of a log fire in the company of others. Having arrived at Aberdaron, there was no certainty, especially in the winter months, of their being able to cross over to Bardsey. They therefore had to stay, sometimes for long periods, at hostelries in the area. One such place was Cwrt, a large homestead which did not pay the usual tithes to the Abbey, but instead gave free board and lodging to those who lived on the island, and their visitors, whilst awaiting favourable weather for a crossing. The last great pilgrimage to Bardsey was undertaken in 1952, under the leadership of the Bishop of Bangor (J.C. Jones).

A picturesque reconstruction of the crossing to Bardsey by a pilgrim, has come down to us from 1846, when two archaelologists visited the island, one of whom was moved to pen the following:

'Once arrived at Aberdaron, the pilgrims would perform their preliminary devotions in St Hywyn's collegiate church, — where now, "The moping owl doth to the moon complain;" or the storm drives through the unglazed casement, and the unshingled roof. Here at all periods, the pilgrims must have been liable to delay; for the strait, between the mainland and the isle, neither does, nor ever did, admit of being crossed in small vessels, at man's will: wind and water must combine to favour the passage, or the transit cannot be attempted. But if detained, they could wander up to the bold head-land looking towards the isle, and there they would find St Mary's chapel open to their prayers for a safe passage, and her mysterious well below high water mark, to test the constancy of their devotions. These spots if visited now, are resorted to only by those who love to see old Ocean in its wildest mood. There they may witness the eternal war of the deep blue billows, fresh from the Atlantic, thundering against the many coloured, many caverned cliffs; there they may look over precipices, hundreds of feet down into the coerulean deep, and extend their gaze for many a fathom beneath its pellucid surface. Far off at sea, between the main-land and Ynys Enlli, they may be aware of the Race rushing and boiling along at ten knots an hour; and if the wind be adverse, breaking into a line of foaming billows that few boats would venture to face. When ready to embark, they would have to go to a circuitous route to the little cave of Porth Meudwy, beneath the Abbey Court-house; and thence, under favourable circumstances, might steal along in a boat under the lofty cliffs till they came to the point of Pen y Cil, where leaving on the right hand the precipice of the Parwyd, shelving six hundred feet down into the sea, they would stretch across for the southern point of the isle. As their bark danced over the waves, the many tribes of sea fowl that frequent the sound, would flit over their heads, or dive for their watery prey even at the very points of the oars: the air and sea would seem pregnant with life; the sturdy boatmen would at times stop to rest, and would offer up a brief oraison: they would then resume their pull, and in two hours, *at the soonest*, they would have finished the passage of only six miles. Once, however, at Bardsey, the difficulty was only half accomplished . . . Those truly, who could get a good wind, for both going and coming back, — or who could find a tranquil time, when the monarch of the air might favour them, — or those who were born under a lucky star, — might, indeed, return the same day: but others have been detained *three weeks* at Bardsey, waiting for a fitting moment, or, if they have ventured into the current, have been carried "Leagues afar, over the stormy main;" and, having started in Caernarvonshire, have landed somewhere on the shores of Cardigan. No doubt, then, as now, other troubles awaited the adventurous pilgrim, to be felt, but not described.'

The days of the abbey were ended in 1536-37, under the Reformation of Henry VIII and the 'dissolution of the monasteries' which took place over the whole of Britain. The Abbey and all its lands and property came into the hands of the long established family of John Wynn of Bodfel in 1553. John Wynn, as we have seen before, was to use the island for very different purposes to those of the Black Canons. In 1569, he was accused by a member of another prominent family in Llŷn, that of Cefnamlwch, in the court of 'Star Chamber' of being 'a man of evil disposition, chief captain and sole supporter, defender and sustainer' of piracy, which was rife at that time in Gwynedd. On Bardsey he kept large supplies of food, meat, bread and drink with which he supplied pirate vessels in return for wines, iron, salt, spices etc. He made a fortune from the exchange and sold goods on the mainland over a large area.

Ynys Enlli (Bardsey Island)

The last of the long line of Bardsey Abbots was one Simon
Conwy, who was the heir to 'Bodnithoedd' near Sarn Mellteyrn.
The best remembered one in folk memory, however is Madog
(15th century) who was known as Madog y Caws ('Madog of the
Cheese'). The story is told that it had come to the ears of one Deio
ap Ieuan Ddu, of Ceredigion (Cardigan), that the Abbot of Bardsey
was 'an exceptionally generous man', and in the hope of
experiencing this generosity, Deio crossed over to the island. He
took with him an offering of a 'Cywydd' (a poem written for a
special occasion in a strict metre), one which was full of praise and
flattery for the Abbot and the monks. But things did not go as well
as he had expected, and during his stay the food he received was not
very appetising. He was given stale bread, maggoty cheese and
sour milk. The magic of Bardsey did not impress itself on Deio. He
burnt his poem, and set about writing another, known to posterity
as 'Awdl y Caws' (ode of the cheese), full of irony and sarcasm. Not

everyone has been enchanted by the Island of the Saints!

After the demise of the Abbey on Bardsey and its associations with piracy, it became home to a fishing/farming community, however, it always maintained in the eyes of this community a deep religious reverence. Thomas Pennant in the 1770's makes this observation:

> 'From this port (Aberdaron) I once took boat for Bardseye [sic] island, which lies about three leagues to the west. The mariners seemed tinctured with the piety of the place; for they had not rowed far, before they made a full stop, pulled off their hats, and offered up a short prayer.'

Mr Bingley, who visited the island at the end of the 18th century, makes the following interesting remarks on one of the subsistence methods used by the islanders. Referring to the mountainous end of the island, he says:

'Among these precipices the intrepid inhabitants, in the spring of the year, employ themselves in collecting the eggs of various species of sea-fowl that frequent them. This usually done bare footed, to prevent them slipping from heights whence were they to fall they must be dashed to pieces; and their concern for their safety, while seizing these eggs, is infinitely less than that of the beholder:

> Nor untrembling canst thou see
> How from a scraggy rock, whose prominence
> Half o'ershades the ocean, hardy men,
> Fearless of dashing waves, do gather them.

These poor fellows do not often meet with accidents, except by the giving way of pieces of the rock. In this case they are irrecoverably lost. The men who venture without ropes are accounted by the natives the most bold climbers: those who are more cautious fix a rope about their middle which is held by some persons on the top of the rock. By this they slip down to the place where they think the greatest number of eggs are to be found; untying the rope from their body, they fasten it to the basket that is to contain the eggs, which they carry in their hand. When this is filled, they make a signal to their companions to draw them up.'

Bingley goes on to observe:

'Till about forty years ago, no sparrows had been known to breed here; three nests were, however, built during the same spring, and the produce have since completely colonised the place.

The number of inhabitants is 84. The sheep are small and very wild.

In the year 1821 a lighthouse was erected on this island, the light of which is 146 feet above high water mark at spring tides.'

In a guide book of 1878 the number of inhabitants was described as being 'around 60'. Not long afterwards it seems that there was a population increase on Bardsey, for in 1907 there were:

'90 inhabitants whose occupations are fishing, collecting the eggs of sea birds, and trafficking in the skins of rabbits.'

Bardsey came into the possession of the Newborough family through Sir John Wynn ab Hugh, of Bodfel. It was the 3rd Lord Newborough who instigated the tradition of the 'King of Bardsey'. This man was set up to 'rule' his island kingdom, it was thought appropriate that with the island being remote it would be a good idea for someone to be in a position of responsibility. The 'kingship' was supposed to remain in one particular family and remained an institution for many generations. The last 'king' was Love Pritchard who died in 1926. After his death the islanders continued to elect a 'president'. This practise continued probably for as long as the community remained on Bardsey.

In the case of the manor of Bardsey there were extensive manorial lands on the mainland in the area of Aberdaron and Uwchmynydd. This manorial holding was described in the Agreement of 1252, between the Abbot of Bardsey and the secular canons of Aberdaron (already referred to) as the 'abadaeth'. According to a couple of surveys which were done in Tudor times — one in 1537, the other in 1592 — the abadaeth consisted of four townships: Uwchsely, Issely, Ultradaron and Tremorfa. A 'township' was simply an area designated in mediaeval times for administrative purposes, it was an area occupied by a few hamlets, scattered farms and smallholdings. It in no way equates with the modern concept of a town.

Uwchsely, occupied the tip of the peninsula, with its eastern limit marked by the Afon Saint. Ultradaron spread in a thin coastal strip from Aberdaron eastwards almost as far as Rhiw. Issely lay between the Saint and the Daron rivers and was bordered on the north by Tremorfa, which was in roughly the same area as that occupied presently by Bryncroes and Llangwnnadl, this was the northern boundary of the abadaeth.

All manors had their courts, where disputes between landholders and peasants would be heard and adjudged. Mostly, these cases had to do with land division and livestock, rents and dues etc. Murder, injury and theft were rare, though not unknown. As a reminder of this, there is a field just up the road from Cwrt (described later) called Bryn Crocbren. Close by, is the 'field of weeping' where mourners for the recently-hanged would gather. Close by is the 'whipping field'. Incidentally, the site for the gallows was chosen so that the latest victim, swinging in the breeze, would be visible over most of the manor-lands of Bardsey as a warning to potential wrongdoers.

In 1547 the 'court' is described as a 'house withein walls nygh the said Ile called the Cort of Bardesey with orchard and garden romes and courts containing by estimation 2 acres'. The report also mentions that in the neighbourhood of the court there were also 157 acres of land belonging to it, comprising arable, pasture, and meadow and including an item of 'furzy' land, partly arable, measuring 6 acres called Tredom. Tredom was mentioned in the Agreement of 1252.

It was more usual for the court to be at the manorial administrative centre, but in the case of Bardsey, being so isolated, it was thought that the court would be better placed on the mainland.

[4] There is evidence at Bychestyn of a farming settlement of possibly 15th or 16th century. There are field boundaries in the area of gorse and heather between the present footpath and the cliff top. Although there is not a lot to see due to this vegetation, aerial photographs show the marks clearly. The fields are divided up into strips or 'quillets', each strip being tended by one individual much in the way of the traditional mediaeval 'open field system'. These mediaeval-style holdings were still the norm in 1592, when a survey of the lands owned by the Abbey of Bardsey was carried out. Probably associated with these fields is a rectangular enclosure on Mynydd Bychestyn (a hill on the edge of the field system on the Aberdaron side), it measures 40 yards by 25 yards with remains of a hut about 15 feet square, which may have been clay or turf built.

[5] 'Cwrt' as its name suggests, was once a court house. In fact it was the court for the manor of Bardsey. A manor in mediaeval and later times (up to late Tudor times when the 'manorial system' started to die out) was a holding of land over a wide area covering, sometimes, many parishes and villages. The inhabitants of these areas would pay tithes and dues to the 'lord of the manor'. These would be paid in produce or labour. Produce tithes were usually paid in oats and barley, measures of oats and barley varied from district to district. In western Llŷn the measure of the 'hobad' (or hobet) was used:

2 sackfuls + 1 hobad + 4 bushels
½ sackful + 1 telad + 2 bushels
¼ sackful + hanner telad + 1 bushel

1 hanner telad of Barley weighed 56l lbs
1 hanner telad of Oats weighed 421 lbs

In this area, these tithes and dues were called 'porthiant'.

[6] Ffynnon Saint is a small 'D' shaped pool about 3' across surrounded by stone walling below water-level. It has an iron lid at ground level — not now visible. There is a 1' high dry stone wall surrounding the well on three sides leaving it open to the west.

Aberdaron tradition says that moles are never found on the Uwchmynydd side of Afon Saint!

— ROAD

--- FOOTPATH

(1), (2) etc. NUMBERS FOR HISTORICAL NOTES

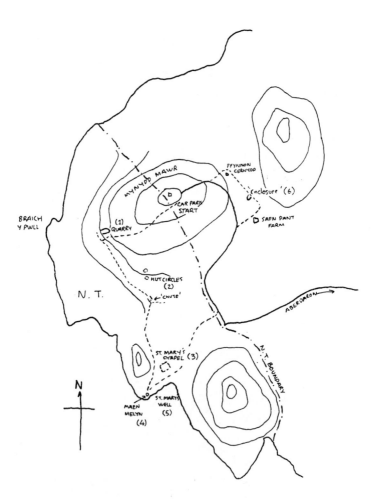

Mynydd Mawr — Capel Mair

1½ hours

Quite an easy walk with some fine views over Ynys Enlli and the surrounding area. If you have dogs with you keep them under strict control here, as there are a lot of sheep about, and the gorse and heather tends to hide them until you are beside them.

Start from the look-out point on the top of Mynydd Mawr, up which you can drive and park.

Look towards Ynys Enlli (*Bardsey*) and head in that direction onto a concrete path which will lead you down the hillside in its direction. There are fine views of the island and its monastery from here.

Continue down the path until you see some large and clearly defined quarry workings on your right.[1] In a few metres you will come to a path which crosses yours, continue on over this until the next grass path where you will turn left.

Quarry entrance

A short while after the quarry, you will come to a large outcrop of rock on your left, if you head up past this rock for a couple of hundred metres heading N.N.W., you will come to the remains of two hut circles on map ref: (SH 2885, 3250).[2]

Retrace your steps to the path and in about 20 metres, keeping Bardsey on your right, you will see below you the remains of St Mary's chapel surrounded by low walls.[3]

In the opposite direction to Aberdaron is a path leading off in the direction of the island. Make your way, taking care down the rocks, onto this path.

You will now be heading towards a rocky cove in front of you with the island on your right. As you pass a large outcrop of rock, turn towards Enlli and head in that direction to a standing stone called Maen Melyn ('yellow stone') on Trwyn Maen Melyn ('yellow stone point').[4]

With the island behind you, make your way to the rocky cove on your right where in a little while you will come to some stone steps, these lead down to Ffynnon Fair ('St Mary's well'),[5] take care here if you wish to view the site.

After returning to the top of the steps, and with the island on your left, head towards Capel Mair ('St Mary's chapel').

With the island behind you, head left around the hill in front of you and make your way towards the roadway at the top, keeping the island behind you all the way.

On emerging onto this tarmaced road, turn left and head uphill until the road swings sharply to the left, at this point you will leave the road and walk alongside the fence on a small footpath.

In a short distance the fence will drop away to your right but you continue along the path, noting that the fields in the distance towards the sea are long and narrow. These are known as quillets and are ancient field boundaries, more or less unchanged from the days when they were made.

Keeping this wall on your left follow the path along the wall. You are now heading towards Ffynnon Cernydd, in around a hundred metres you will see it set in a three sided enclosure open to the east.

Set off now to return to your car on the top of Mynydd Mawr.

Head up the hill behind the well until you meet the road, turn right and follow this to the end.

History notes

[1] This rather scenically situated quarry is probably of the 19th century, the track which leads from its 'mouth' in the direction of Aberdaron was constructed by the quarry men for the transport of the quarry produce, there would have been a constant 'to-ing and fro-ing' of carts loaded with rock being pulled by men, mules or donkeys. There is an interesting feature to look out for where the track terminates on the edge of a rock bluff; if you look down to the foot of the bluff where the track, winding off to the left, is clearly visible you will see a well defined 'chute' in the rock face. This is where the carts would have been tipped at the top of the bluff and the contents tumbled down to the bottom to be reloaded on other carts for the next stage of the journey. The constant rolling of rocks down this steep slope has gouged out the 'chute' now visible.

[2] These two hut circles, around 50 metres apart, are an indication of an isolated farming settlement. As has been previously stated in another walk, to accurately date these kind of remains is practically impossible as dwellings of this sort were the norm from the Celtic Iron Age period, through the centuries of the Roman occupation and well into the Dark Ages. The broad flattish area below them — on which the remains of St Mary's chapel now stands (referred to shortly), may have been an area cultivated by these remote-living pastoralists — geographically and chronologically. This flatish area surprisingly, is often sheltered from the sea winds and it may not have been impossible for some hardy cereal crops to be grown here. It is also conceivable that animals such as sheep and goats, when not being allowed to roam free over the surrounding hills and mountains, could be corralled here in wattle or timber enclosures. A picture comes to mind when looking at a site like this of what a Dark Age 'farm' would have been like, an unbelievably austere existence by modern standards, yet all basic human requirements such as food, water and shelter would not necessarily have been in

short supply. The dwellings occupied by these farming families are now represented by often poorly defined remains, such as those on this site. These were constructed by the erection of a rough stone wall vaguely circular, between ⅔ and 1 metre high, surrounding a sunken, beaten-earth floor. The roof would have been constructed in a 'teepee' fashion with long poles resting on the top of the stone wall rising up to an apex. The poles would have been covered over with either thatch, bracken, turf, or any combination thereof. There would have been a single entrance with a pole set in the ground at either side to support a leather door flap. The walls of the building would be draught proofed with mud and moss. In the summer, the hearth for cooking would be situated outside, but during the winter it would obviously be inside in the centre of the hut, the smoke would find its way out through holes and chinks in the roof. Inside there would be no 'furniture' of any kind, people would sit on the floor and beds were simply piles of straw or heather etc., on the floor. The fire would occupy the centre of the hut. Cooking and eating utensils would be simple and made of wood, wickerwork, leather or unfired clay. Hut circles such as these show much variation in size, between about 3mtrs and 9mtrs in diameter, no doubt the number of intended occupants would govern the size of the construction. A site such as this, with two small huts, would maybe represent the farming settlement of a single family.

[3] The remains now visible, are of a building around 12 mtrs by 7 mtrs, surrounded by an enclosure roughly 84 square mtrs. The footings of this building have been dug out, some of the loose stones which would have been incorporated in the wall show signs of having been mortared. The enclosure, which surrounds the church remains, is a good example of an area of mediaeval cultivation. Indeed, William Williams (1738-1817) says: 'The plain in which it is situated is divided into a vast number of quillets (strips) which belong to as many different proprietors.' If indeed this plot of land was cultivated in the Dark Ages, possibly by the dwellers in the previously mentioned huts on the higher ground nearby, it would demonstrate a continuance of cultivation from the

5th, 6th & 7th centuries through the middle ages and probably into the 16th century and the Tudor period.

Site of Capel Mair ('St Mary's chapel')

The earliest record of the remains as those of a church are of 1748. Interestingly, a late 18th century drawing shows the ruins of a typical 17th century house. However, it must be supposed that a church of some sort has been on this site since early mediaeval times at least. Exactly what it was like wo do not know; one description states that it was 11 mtrs long by 4½ mtrs wide, not including the several dormitories that pertained to it. If this description is correct it is possible to visualise this as a small abbey which would have provided accommodation for pilgrims to Ynys Enlli (*'Bardsey'*). One can picture then, a small huddle of thatched stone buildings occupied by a few monks, possibly, largely self sufficient, growing a few crops on the surrounding cultivated enclosure, maybe with a few sheep on the adjacent hillsides.

Maen Melyn

[4] This stone although leaning to one side is nevertheless a standing-stone, placed here by Man in the Neolithic or Bronze Age.

Standing stones; what are they? what were they? Erected in Neolithic and Early Bronze Age times, enigmatic fingers of stone, placed seemingly at random over the whole of Britain, over Europe and with equivalents in many part of the world, but erected for what purpose? Archaelologists mostly suggest that they marked the sites of burials, indeed burials have been found under or close to some of them, but most, on excavation, have proved to be unconnected with any burials. So it would seem that this was not their function, what then was it? If you are equipped with a ruler or any other straight edged implement and an Ordinance Survey map of virtually any area of Britain, and then locate the sites of all the standing stones marked on the map you will notice after only a few minutues work that you are able to line up many in various criss-crossing straight lines. Obviously, some of the alignments thus produced can be explained by chance, but usually, after a little diligence and perseverance with the map, very many more lines can be found than can be accounted for by chance. What you have found are examples of the controversial 'ley lines'. You may also notice that churches may appear in these alignments, indeed, any site which is demonstrably ancient i.e., prehistoric, will often be found to form straight lines with other such sites. It should be borne in mind that the vast majority, if not all old churches, are placed on pre-existing ancient pagan sacred sites. The policy of the Christian Church in its early years was not to try and establish new sacred sites, but to superimpose a Christian site onto an old pagan one, so that, in the eyes of the common people the old gods had been conquered and superseded by the new, whilst, at the same time continuing the sanctity of the site itself. It is for this reason that so many churches appear on ley lines. Other sites likely to appear on leys include, stone circles, burial mounds, barrows, tumuli, dolmens, cromlechs and any other similar related or equivalent sites. Also included are some distinctive natural features, the most important being mountain tops, or particularly cairns on mountain tops.

This whole concept of ley lines was the 'rediscovery' of one Alfred Watkins in the 1920's. Watkins was an avid countryside rambler and walker and this vision of the countryside laid out in a grid-like pattern reputedly came to him in a moment of inspiration. He published a book called 'The Old Straight Track' and the cult of ley lines, as he called them was born. Needless to say, Watkins did not know what they were, nor do we today, although between his time and ours, rivers of ink have flowed carrying with them theories ranging from the banal to the bizarre. Some theories remain afloat, others sinking without trace, still others caught in eddies and backwaters, often to be flushed out again with a new flood of interest in the subject of ley lines. The explanation offered by Watkins was that these lines were laid down in ancient times as way markers, route finders or trade routes etc. However, as interest in leys developed and more people began to investigate and plot them, and as the number found increased, it was shown that many lines passed straight through lakes, swamps, straight off cliffs and over inaccessible peaks, in short, direct but very inconvenient routes indeed. The way-marker theory has been almost totally abandoned. Modern theories of ley lines revolve around an idea that these lines are energy carriers of some sort, natural earth energy that manifests itself on the earth's surface in straight lines. In the past this energy, so goes the theory, was concentrated in various points by our ancestors, or did so naturally. Then marked by standing stones and such like where the accumulated energy could be used by certain individuals among the people, who were versed in the necessary techniques, for the benefit of the community e.g. helping the growth of crops or in healing the sick — indeed many stones today have folk lore connected with them relating to healing. This whole concept is too esoteric for the acceptance of most archaelologists, the majority of whom do not even accept the existence of alignments in the first place.

Many sites on ley lines have associated folk lore attached to them e.g. stones that move, stones that speak, stones that heal, buried treasure guarded by spirits, burial mounds guarded by serpents and dragons, all of which may be a garbled and distant folk memory of the 'treasure' of the energy which flowed along these lines. It is interesting to note that most people who practice the art of dowsing maintain that the lines are active today. The energy is still there, although the ley system is obviously much mutilated in present times with the destruction of so many ancient sites.

The authors have been able to ascertain that this stone, Maen Melyn, is the culmination (or start) of three ley lines.

[5] In the rocks of the bay, beneath the site of the church, and covered at high tide, is the celebrated Ffynnon Fair. There is a folk-belief attached to this well. To quote Edmund Hyde-Hall:

> 'Below its site (St Mary's church) close upon the edge of the sea and only to be reached by descending a craggy and narrow path, dreadful to the sight and horrible to the imagination, is St Mary's Well, or Ffynnon Fair. The votaries who can bring

to the chapel a mouthful of water, unspilled and unswallowed, may be secure of their wishes' accomplishment; but it must be no ordinary object of cupidity or ambition which could tempt an inland-bred man to the experiment, however ardent his wish or strong his faith.'

There is a slight variation on this legend which appears in an early 20th century guide book:

'The other supposed object of special interest is Ffynnon Fair, 'Our Lady's Well', which occupies a hollow in the cliff a little to the right of the bottom of the rock staircase . . . and is only accessible at low tide. It is a little basin of freshwater filled by a tiny stream trickling down the rock and is about two feet deep. The pilgrim who was skillful enough to convey a palmful to the top of the cliff without spilling any had his fondest wishes granted. On the rock beside the well is the impression of "Our Lady's" hand, also of the shoe of her horse.'

Other slight variants on the legend state that the bearer of the water, on ascending to the church should then pass three times around it, also without spilling/swallowing a drop, before his wishes are granted.

[6] This enclosure with its associated small building, possibly a house, may date from mediaeval times and represent another example of an agricultural settlement in this remote spot.

RHIW

Before we take you off the beaten track and lead you to ancient battle grounds, where Arthur fought his last battle with Mordred, let us first take you through the history of this once important region:

The whole area of Rhiw has been extensively populated from as early as the Neolithic period, and remains such as the axe factory and cromlechs (mentioned in a later walk), date from then. There are standing stones, enigmatic representatives of the Bronze Age. There are two Iron Age hillforts and numerous roundhut settlement sites from Roman and Dark Age times. There is evidence of occupation and cultivation through the middle ages and into the Tudor and Modern eras. So in ancient times the Rhiw area was something of a centre of population and occupation, somewhat in contrast to its rather 'backwater' status of today.

We can catch a few faint glimpses of the history of Rhiw from the later Dark Ages and the mediaeval period. The Lewis family, who, in Tudor times were the squires of Plas-yn-Rhiw — which is the National Trust property just off the road, as it begins its climb up to the village from the direction of Hell's Mouth. This family traditionally traces its descent back to the ninth century, to King Merfyn Frych of Gwynedd. During the tenth century, this part of the coast along with most other parts, was subject to raids by Vikings and in order to assist the people of Rhiw in the defence of their lands, Merfyn Frych sent his grandson Meirion Goch and some wariors to settle here. Plas-yn-Rhiw is thought to be the location of the homestead of Meirion.

Also in the immediate neighbourhood of Plas-yn-Rhiw, was situated in mediaeval times, a tribal hamlet. A farmstead just below Plas-yn-Rhiw bears in its name a reference to one Heili, who was possibly a clan chieftain of this time. This small settlement was another example of a bond-township, paying tribute in produce or money to the lord of the manor, as well as looking after his horses or hounds — during the fourteenth century the lord was the same Nigel de Loryng who exacted dues from the peasants of Neigwl township. Two families stood out from the common herd in this small community. All the bond families were obliged, at a cost, to have their corn ground at the lord's mill, these two families were permitted to grind their corn at their own mill in Rhiw. This is an example of the often mixed nature of some townships of the middle ages between bondsmen and freemen, it seems that these two families, headed by Einion and Bleddyn were free families, exempt from all dues to the lord of the manor. It was from men and families such as this, that during the Tudor period small estates began to be put together by freemen, with bits and pieces of land acquired by various means and assembled into one holding.

St Aelrhiw's church

The Parish church of St Aelrhiw

This church is probably the site of the original Llan or ecclesiastical settlement of St Aelrhiw in the sixth century. The present building, however, only dates from the 18th century, but is constructed on the site of an earlier church. A north east doorway is reputedly Norman. There was extensive restoration work done in 1860-1. Behind the font, set in the west wall is an upright gravestone, bearing a coat of arms and a skull-and-crossbones, and is inscribed: 'Here leith the body of Lowry, the fifth daughter and heiress of Thomas ap Richard of Bodwythog, Gent, and the wife of Frederick Wynne. Shee died the 8 of August Anno Din 1674, and also ye body of ye said Frederick Wynne, the sonne of John Wynne of Bodfean who died . . . .' This Frederick Wynne was a church warden in 1672 and presented the church with a pewter flagon which dates from 1662 as well as a silver chalice. The flagon somehow got lost and turned up in the possession of the Nanhoron family who re-presented it to the church sometime in the early part of this century. In the small vestry is an old oak chest, dated 1715 and initialled W:R.H:W.I.

During the Great War many bodies were washed ashore at Porth Neigwl, some were interred in the graveyard here, one was Thomas Pengilly, of Clovelley, North Devon, whose body came ashore on May 17,1917.

The bell is dated 1670 and has the initials R.P.R:F.W.W:T.W; upon it.

Our old friend Edmund Hyde Hall was not much impressed with this church, he says:

> 'The church is a small, dark, mean building without even a pulpit, and in no respect well kept. Near it stands the parsonage, a very wretched building also, meanly thatched, quite unprotected, and, forming altogether a very dreary abode.'

About 150 metres south west of the church stands 'Ffynnon Aelrhiw' (St Aelrhiw's well) it is set into a steep hillside. The well is enclosed by a wall almost 3 metres square with an entrance on the north east. The well has been incorporated in a later field wall.

Plas-yn-Rhiw

This house dates from the early 1600's, originally with two storeys and a loft, it was extended to the north west in the 18th century, with alterations in the 19th century. There is a 19th century reproduction of a date plate (I.L.1634) over the groundfloor window on the east front of the house, it may be a re-make of the original and therefore be the date of the house's building. To the south of the house is an 18th century 'crogloft' cottage which was, at one time, used as a bake-house and wash-house.

There are other ruined outbuildings to the north of the house and these are of the 18th and 19th centuries.

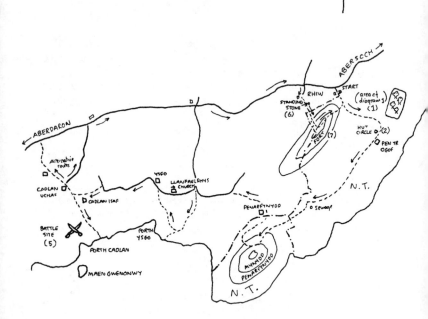

- ROAD
--- FOOTPATH
(1). (2) etc. NUMBERS FOR HISTORICAL NOTES

N

ABERSOCH

RHIW
START
(area of diagram)
(1)

STANDING STONE
(6)

ABERDARON

HUT CIRCLE ● (2)

PEN YR OGOF

FORK (7)

N.T.

YSGO

LLANFAELRHYS CHURCH

Alternative routes

CADLAN UCHAF

CADLAN ISAF

PENARFYNYDD

SEWAGE

BATTLE SITE (5)

PORTH YSGO

PORTH CADLAN

MAEN GWENONWY

MYNYDD PENARFYNYDD

N.T.

138

Walk 9

Rhiw — Porth Cadlan

4 hours

History and walking are what this book is about and in this walk you will literally be walking in the footsteps of King Arthur and his last battle before he was taken to Afallon ('Avalon'), Ynys Enlli ('Bardsey') to be healed. Fairly easy walk with some fine views.

As there are no official car parks in this village, park where you can at the cottage called Pen-y-Groes, approximately 300 metres along the road from the crossroads in Rhiw village when heading towards Abersoch, nearly at the end of the village. Map reference: SH 2284, 2777.

Take the lane that forms a 'T' junction with the main road at Pen-y-Groes and head along this track until the first gate, enter this, heading down the slope, keeping alongside the dry-stone wall to your left.

This path leads past three terraced cottages, the first of which is called Bay View. After a short walk, about 200 metres, meet up with another gate, go through this and keep heading downhill.

After the first bend in the lane, look over the wall, in this field are many ancient remains.[1]

Immediately after passing the next cottage, Pant, turn right and follow this track towards the wall in front of you, about 300 metres, with small ruined cottage close by.[2] On reaching the wall turn left at its top corner and follow it past the cottage called Pen-yr-ogof. Continue along this track, passing some old sheep folds and continue around the hillside — which incidentally is the site of an old fortified homestead that we will be visiting on the return.

Keep on this path until at the end of the hill the path makes a right turn towards a stile, go over this and turn left through the gate passing the pumping station on your left and continue on to the

139

next stile.

You are now heading towards the 'trig point' on Mynydd Penarfynydd, height: 177 metres. On reaching this, you will have a vantage point over the islands including Bardsey. The one closest to you is called Maen Gwenonwy, the two further out are, Ynys Gwylan Fawr and Ynys Gwylan Fach — large gull island and small gull island. Interspersed amid the bracken and gorse on Penarfynydd headland are further examples of round hut settlements but they are very difficult to detect: Penarfynydd is the site of a mediaeval township.

As this area is open land with no discernible paths, you must trust our directions from here to the path, which is about 200 metres away. Face towards Ynys Enlli ('*Bardsey*'), due west, and walk in that direction until you cross a path, turn right onto this and follow it until you reach the gate into the farm yard at Penarfynydd Farm. After entering the yard, head towards the exit, cross the lane and immediately into a field keeping to the right of the fence.

Head along this 'tractor track', until after a while the path will cross to the other side of the fence — you may hit problems here in wet weather as the field you are entering gets quite boggy, if this is the case, stay on your side of the fence and continue until you reach the stile in the corner of the field, cross this and here you will emerge onto a road, turn left and follow this.

Keep on this road taking the centre of a triple fork and continue on until you come to a stream which runs under the road, at this point, follow the footpath sign and turn sharp left onto a path which runs beside the stream and on through a kissing gate.

Detour[3]

At the crossroads, where the stream runs under the road, you can if you like take a short detour for about 300 metres to an old church, Llanfaelrhys. Cross over the stream and head uphill where you will come across the church on your right.

Retrace your steps, then take the footpath which leaves the road at the sharp bend and heads down a valley called Nant-y-Gadwen (chain valley).[4] In a short while the path crosses a small bridge where you will have a choice of high or low paths.

Sunset over the manganese mines

At the end of the valley you will come to a kissing gate, go through this, you are now within the National Trust property of Porth Ysgo. Head along this path skirting the hillside on your right and keeping to the right.

As you round the hillside you will be overlooking Maen Gwenonwy. On your left is a path that runs down to the secluded and very attractive beach which is popular with the tourists, it features a waterfall that cascades almost on to the beach.

If you are not going on to the beach, follow the path up the hill and over the bridge, which you will come to in a few hundred metres, crossing the stile in front of you, make your way onto the tarmaced road and turn left, walking past the farm yard duck pond on your right. In a few hundred metres you will come upon a footpath sign for Porth Cadlan, cross this stile.

After crossing this stile head along the wall on your right until the next stile and continue, heading towards the visible stiles. At the stile just before the farm, you will see across the small valley in front of you the supposed site of King Arthur's last battle.[5]

You will need to pass the farm on your left heading towards the stile situated just after the barn, turn right and head along the farm track until the large gate where you will cross the stile into the fields heading towards the stream, you will need to cross this and then turn left following the stream until the last stile where you emerge onto the rough land above the sea, turn right and walk a few metres where in front of you is a large rock, this becomes an Island at high tide, and is known as Maen Gwenonwy.

Retrace your steps to the stile at the gate and turn left along the track turning right at the junction in a few metres. Follow this farm track until it meets the main road where you will turn right and continue along this road until the crossroads at Rhiw.

At the crossroads at Rhiw turn right, and in about 30 metres turn left, where on your left 30 metres up the lane you will see embedded in the wall a standing stone.[6]

Continue up the lane until you reach the cottage called 'Terfyn Isaf' where after turning sharp right, cross the stile in front of you, turn immediately left and walk along the wall until in a few metres you will come to another stile which you will cross and turn right following the wall uphill to the stile at the rocks.

Cross this and make your way up the rocks on your left. You are standing on top of Mynydd y Graig ('craggy mountain'), and the site of an early settlement.[7]

Keeping fairly close to the edge of the escarpment make your way, heading in the direction of the Bay, where at the first opportunity you will leave the crags and make your way down to the foot of the rocks heading towards the drystone wall, at which you will turn right, following the wall into the corner of the field and to the gate. After going through this follow the path back to your car.

History notes
[1] The field over the wall on the left hand side which slopes down towards a small wood, is an area which contains many features

which show that this area was one of occupation and agriculture from prehistoric to modern times.

Visible in the lower half of the field are the remains of ancient terracing — simply a method of levelling sections of sloping land to facilitate its cultivation. Associated with this system of terraced fields are round huts and long huts. It is generally agreed among archaeologists that round huts predate long huts. It would appear that this field terracing is associated with the round huts, which may indicate a pre-Roman date. The fields would undoubtedly have been used by the subsequent builders of the long huts, these may, tentatively, be dated to the later Dark Ages or very early mediaeval period.

It appears that the area was abandoned during the mediaeval period proper, but that occupation and cultivation re-commenced in comparatively recent times, as exemplified by the ruins of the cottage and its associated corrals and sheep folds.

As there are numerous features of interest in this field, it is proposed to display them on a plan (fig.1)

1. (a) and (b) are animal corrals associated with the old cottage (no. 4).

2. Site of round hut approximately 6 metres across.

3. 100 metres south east of (2) round hut, similar size. Adjacent to this is the possible later site of a long hut.

4. Old cottage, this may also occupy the former site of a long hut. It had opposing doorways, which is a primitive feature reminiscent of a mediaeval hall house.

5. A masonry-walled well about 1 metre in diameter with an open 'forecourt'. This is incorporated in a modern field wall and there is no evidence of any religious usage, but such usage is entirely possible given the emphasis placed upon this natural spring by having a wall built round it which is not necessary for the mere collection of water. This well, or at least the wall around it, is probably contemporary with nearby ruined buildings e.g. 1 & 4.

6. Remains of field terracing, probably contemporary with round huts.

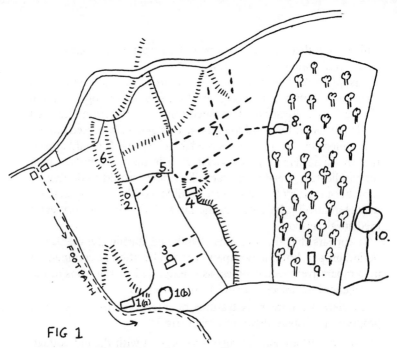

FIG 1

HUTS AND FIELD SYSTEMS AT RHIW

7. Field boundaries possibly contemporary with 1, 4 & 5.

8. A 'platform house' 9 metres long with an associated enclosure, possibly of early mediaeval date.

9. An ancient enclosure some 12 metres long and 6 metres wide with walls of piled stone, 1 to 1.3 metres thick. This is probably older than the abandoned enclosures near it, which, may be contemporary with the old cottage.

10. An enclosure which may be the remains of a group of round huts. On the north wall is a rectangular building like a platform house 8 metres by nearly 5 metres with a doorway 1.5 metres wide on the north side. Its walls are 1 to 1.2 metres thick, it would appear that this long hut is later in date than the associated enclosure. It is possible that the builder sited his dwelling where he did, in order to utilise the already existing enclosure wall which may have surrounded earlier round hut dwellings.

Ruined cottage with hut circle' (Hut circle on right of picture between cottage and wall)

2 This is a nice example of continuity of land use: If you look towards the small ruined cottage which is probably around three hundred years old, just in front of it you will notice a circular group of stones around 5 metres across. This is the remains of a round-hut of possible middle Dark Age date, i.e. 7th to 9th century. Despite its ancient date and dilapidated appearance this cottage was in a habitable condition until around 1980.

3 Llanfaelrhys Church

St Maelrhys was a cousin to Cadfan who founded the monastery on Ynys Enlli (*Bardsey*) and also a cousin to Hywyn who founded the church at Aberdaron. The existing fabric of the church, is in part mediaeval, but the slate roof, bell-cote and all openings are modern. It appears from internal jointing that the chancel was added to the mediaeval nave, but there is no clue as to the date at which this occurred. The head of the north door is also probably mediaeval.

The prominent belcot has traditionally been used as a guiding mark for Aberdaron fishermen out in the bay. Around 1800, Llanfaelrhys was an extensive parish serving 224 people and for its size the churchyard reputedly contains more gravestone epitaphs than any other in Llŷn. A large proportion of these date from the period 1758 to 1767. Buried here are several persons who were drowned and washed ashore during the Great War.

Inside, there is a communion table of the early 18th century. The octagonal font is 15th century. The seating with a 'Nanhoron' inscription is of the mid 19th century. It is interesting that this church is the only one dedicated to Maelrhys in the whole of Britain.

[4] On either side of Nant-y-Gadwen are the visible remains of mine workings. These operations were in search of manganese and had commenced around 1827, where 50 men were employed here by 1840. Ore found here, was sent by ship to Liverpool. Between 1894-1945, 196,770 tons of ore were raised, the bulk of it during the periods of the two World Wars.

Porth Cadlan and Maen Gwenonwy,
with battle site on fields above (top right)

⁵ Porth Cadlan, and the fields above it, Cadlan Uchaf and Cadlan Isaf (upper and lower), is poised to become one of the principal sites of historic interest in the whole of Britain! How so? Well, in a recently published book, meticulously researched and convincingly presented material strongly suggests that the last battle of King Arthur was fought against his mortal enemy Mordred on this spot! The book, 'Journey to Avalon', by Chris Barber and David Pykitt is a thorough reconstruction of the historical Arthur, precisely locating the sites of his fabled twelve battles, and in addition the site of his thirteenth and famous last battle, that of Camlan. A couple of chapters are devoted to the part of the story connected with the scene here at Cadlan. There have been, in the past, vast libraries of books published purporting to tell the 'final truth' about King Arthur, many typewriter ribbons have expired in the line of duty in an attempt to disentangle the warp and weft of the legend and historicity of Arthur. Most historians, at least those with the 'establishment' viewpoint, have long since decided that any meaningful reconstruction of events surrounding Arthur is impossible. They view successive attempts by amateurs and professionals alike with disdain, admittedly with some justification, and it must be conceded that in some cases the theories put forward, and not all by amateurs, are just plain daft! However, this latest book says it all, it ties in everything and is thoroughly believable.

Briefly the evidence according to Chris Barber and David Pykitt which places Arthur's last battle here is as follows:

Firstly some place name evidence, Cadlan means 'battle field' or 'place of battle'. The form of an old Welsh word 'Cadgamlan' meaning a rout, could be shortened to either 'Camlan' or 'Cadlan'. The large detached rock at the end of Porth Cadlan, reachable at low-water is called Maen Gwenonwy, 'Gwenonwy's stone'. Gwenonwy was a sister of Arthur. The river-valley a couple of hundred yards away, leading down to Porth Ysgo is called Nant-y-Gadwen.

There is also genealogical evidence which connects Arthur with this area. The sixth century was a time of intense activity by the

Celtic 'saints' on the whole of the western sea-board of Britain, as far south as Armorica (Brittany), north to Scotland and westwards to Ireland. These saints play a part in linking Arthur with this area.

Arthur's sister Gwenonwy married Gwyndaf Hen (the old). One of their sons was Hywyn, founder of Aberdaron church, this makes Hywyn a nephew of Arthur. Gwyddno, a brother of Gwyndaf Hen, had a son Maelrhys, founder of Llanfaelrhys church. Gwen Teirbron, brother also to Gwyddno and Gwyndaf Hen, married Eneas Lydewig and had a son Cadfan, this was the same Cadfan who became first Abbot of Bardsey. So Hywyn, Maelrhys and Cadfan were cousins. Another brother of Gwyndaf Hen, Alan Fyrgan (white heels) is mentioned in the mediaeval book of traditional welsh stories, the Mabinogion as leader of the 'Three Faithless Warbands of the Island of Britain'. It seems he was deserted by them and fought at the battle of Camlan, where he was killed accompanied only by his servants. The father of Gwyndaf Hen, Gwyddno, Gwen Teirbron and Alan Fyrgan was Emyr Llydaw — a king in Amorica, who, in conjunction with Einion — then 'king' of Llŷn and commemorated at Llanengan church — is said to have established some sort of monastic settlement on Bardsey. This would obviously be prior to the recognised establishment of Cadfan in c.516 Einion, incidentally was great-grandson to Cunedda Wledig, founder, with numerous sons, of the kingdom of Gwynedd, after the demise of the Romans in the early 5th century.

Arthur had another sister, Anna who married an Armorican prince, Amwn Ddu (the black) — another son of Emyr Llydaw. They had two sons, Tydecho, a saintly companion of Cadfan, and Samson who was a so-called knight of Arthur's court and has church dedications in Cornwall. Tydecho and Samson were also cousins to Hywyn, Maelrhys, and Cadfan.

The historical Arthur is reputedly descended from a Roman Emperor, Magnus Maximus, rendered into Welsh as Macsen Wledig (Wledig — prince, ruler). There is a story in the Mabinogion called 'The Dream of Macsen Wledig', in which, to cut a long story short, he falls asleep while hunting and dreams of a

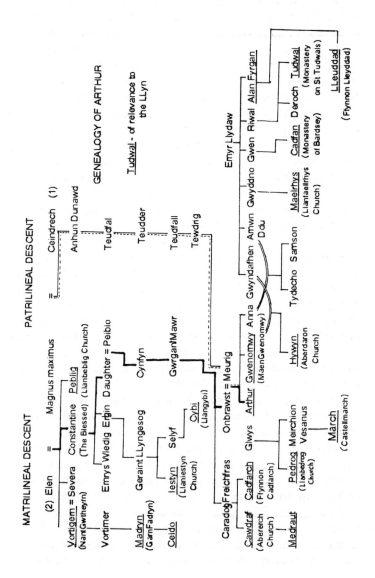

GENEALOGY OF ARTHUR

MATRILINEAL DESCENT   PATRILINEAL DESCENT

149

fair land with a coloured castle containing a fair maiden, he cannot rest until he has found this land, castle and maiden, which turn out to be North Wales, Caernarfon Castle, and his future wife. Caernarfon Castle as it stands today did not exist in the time of Arthur. The stories constituting the mabinogion were put together in mediaeval times, and reflect the situation as it was then. However, when the castle was built by Edward 1, the decorative stone work may have been included with the description of the coloured castle in mind. One of the sons of Macsen is Constantine, or Cystennin Fendigaid (The Blessed), who returns to Wales after his father's death as a 'saint', he has a church dedicated in Caernarfonshire at Llangystennin. Constantine had a daughter who married Peibio and a lineal descent via Cynfyn, and Gwrgant Mawr, arrives at Onbrawst who married Meurig ap Tewdrig. Their offspring was Arthur.

If you will bear with us a while longer in this genealogical maze there is another interesting side branch of family relations. Going back to Constantine. As well as his daughter he also had a son, Erbin, who in turn had a son Geraint Llyngesog (the fleet owner). This Geraint operated a fleet of six-score ships in the Severn estuary, patrolling the coast against Saxon invaders. Geraint married Gwyar, who bore five sons, Cadwy, Iestyn, Selyf, Cyngar and Caw who were cousins to Arthur. Cadwy ruled jointly with Arthur in north-west Somerset, his stronghold was Cadbury Castle. Iestyn established churches in Cornwall, (where he is known as Justin), Anglesey and Llŷn i.e., at Llaniestyn. The son of Cadwy is another Constantine, it was he who took over the reigns of leadership from Arthur after the battle of Camlan.

So it can be seen from this that there is much family connection with Arthur and Llŷn. It is also possible, as well as necessary, to be able to place the other key player in the game, namely Mordred or Medraut, in the area as well. This is achieved as follows:

Caradog Freichfras (the strong armed), was Arthur's Chief Elder at his court, he had two sons, Cawrdaf and Cadfarch. Cawrdaf was also a chief advisor to Arthur, he was also patron of Abererch church near Pwllheli. His brother Cadfarch is commemorated by a well, 'Ffynnon Cadfarch' at the north end of Abererch parish. Cawrdaf had a son Medraut (Mordred), so family connections with Medraut and the Llŷn are clearly demonstrable.

Mordred, as a trusted personage, was appointed as Arthur's regent, he was in charge when Arthur was absent, but obviously somewhere along the line enmity developed between the two. The Mabinogion story of 'Culhwch and Olwen' names Gwenhwyfach as sister to Arthur's Queen Gwenhwyfar (Guinevere). According to early Welsh genealogies, Gwenhwyfach was the wife of Medraut. There seems to have been some animosity between the two women. The Welsh Triads states that Medraut, possibly on Gwenhwyfach's behalf, came to Arthur's court and dragged Gwenhwyfar from her throne and struck her. We are unfortunately, not privy to the reasons behind this assault nor for the sisterly quarrel. Arthur made a retaliatory attack on Medraut's court. In the Triads these are called the first and second of the 'Three Unrestrained Ravaging's of the Island of Britain. These events were undoubtedly contributory to the amimosity which culminated in the battle of Camlan.

Meanwhile the father of Gwenhwyfar, Count Gwrthyr of Leon in Brittany, died in AD 530. Gwenhwyfar inherited his lands and her husband Arthur gained control of these lands which he ruled jointly with an Armorican king named Deroch. In 533 Visigoths invade Deroch's territory and he requested aid from Arthur who was subsequently absent from Britain for four years. In the meantime his regent Medraut seized his realm and Queen. Arthur by now was in Ireland engaged in battle with Llwch Llawinawg, when news of Medraut's treachery reached him. He returned from Ireland with the remnants of his army, and landed at Porth Cadlan, possibly in stormy weather and losing a boat or two, he was awaited by the forces of Medraut. In the ensuing battle (c.537), Medraut was killed and Arthur was critically wounded.

We now come to another intriguing aspect of the story. We need an Avalon! for in the traditional story the wounded Arthur is taken by boat to a nearby island to be healed. Geoffrey of Monmouth, a 12th century chronicler who wrote 'The History of the Kings of

Britain', referred in this to the Island of 'Insula Afallonis' which has been shortened to Avalon. In Welsh versions of the manuscript the name is rendered as 'Ynys Afallach'. In an old book called 'Irish Druids and old Irish Religions' a significant statement is made:

> 'The Welsh Avalon, or the Island of Apples, the everlasting source of the Elixir of Life, the home of Arthur and other mytholical heroes, lay beyond Cardigan bay . . . in the direction of Ireland.'

If you look at a map it is apparent that only one island fits the bill, Bardsey! It is only a relatively short boat journey from the site of the battle of Camlan, boats were present, there was a monastery on Bardsey with a relative of Arthur as Abbot, and presumably, as in most monasteries, some facilities for healing the sick.

After being healed on Bardsey (Avalon), Arthur abdicated in favour of Constantine, the son of his cousin Cadwy. Shortly after this the confederacy of kingdoms set up by Arthur, and effective in resisting the Saxon invasions, disintegrated into its component parts, leaving the way clear for the Saxon's to gain domination of England. The Celts were restricted to the western lands of Cornwall, Wales, Ireland and north into Scotland.

One final interesting note; Jonas, son of Deroch of Armorica (joint ruler with Arthur) is assassinated by one Conomorus. This Conomorus appears in the Arthurian legends, as king Mark of Cornwall and is none other than March ap Meirchion already referred to in connection with Castellmarch in Abersoch.

[6] The large upright stone visible in the wall next to the path is a standing stone of the late Neolithic or early Bronze Age, it has obviously been embodied in the much later field wall. It is quite possible that a few other such standing stones have met a similar fate. This is much more acceptable to the archaeologist or historian if they are utulised in this way or left *in situ*. Unfortunately, very many of these ancient monuments have been removed, broken up, sometimes by farmers, sometimes by pious church goers 'removing offensive pagan symbols', or used in farm buildings with their original positions unrecorded and an important

archaelological site forever lost.

There is another stone, reputedly a standing stone, now in a prone position within a couple of metres down the hill from the first one. There is a legend attached to these stones which commonly occurs throughout Britain with regards standing stones, it goes like this: Two robbers were fleeing from a local church with stolen items and as they crossed the boundary of the two adjoining parishes — marked by the line of this wall, they were instantly turned to stone and here they remain.

[7] This ragged escarpment is called Creigiau Gwineu and is the site of a hillfort, probably of Iron Age date, the builders of this fort skillfully utulised the existing rocky outcrop when building their fortification and this is one reason why it is rather difficult to discern today. The fort is of an elongated oval plan with its main axis following that of the ridge, it is 133 metres in length and up to 63 metres in width. Along the north west side of the fort the natural precipice is the only defence, but the head of a narrow gully has been walled off. The north east end, has a wall built following the contours of the hill, embodying natural rocky features where possible but is now quite ruinous. As stated before it is now difficult to see the man-made remains of this fort. It is divided into two sections or 'wards' by a rough built wall. The remains of three circular huts are visible in the western 'ward'.

It is impossible to say if it continued to be occupied in Roman times, it may have been. It is also possible that it may have been occupied or re-occupied in the sub-Roman, Dark Ages. There have been no datable remains found on this site.

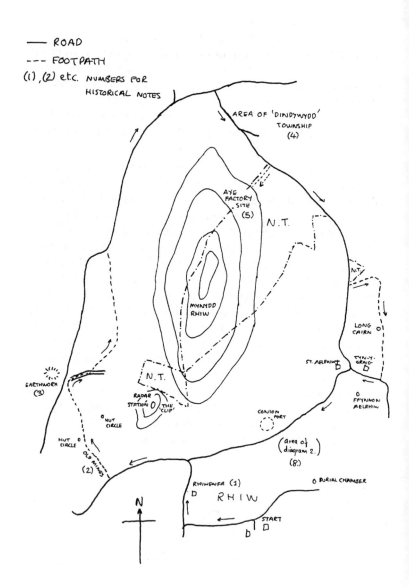

— ROAD

--- FOOTPATH

(1),(2) etc. NUMBERS FOR HISTORICAL NOTES

AREA OF 'DINDYWYDD' TOWNSHIP (4)

AXE FACTORY SITE (5)

N.T.

MYNYDD RHIW

N.T.

EARTHWORK (3)

N.T.

LONG CAIRN o

ST. AELRHIW

TYN-Y-GRAIG

O FFYNNON AELRHIW

RADAR STATION o THE CLIP

N.T.

o HUT CIRCLE

HUT CIRCLE o

OLD MINES (2)

CONION FORT

(area of diagram 2.) (8.)

RHIWENFA (1)

RHIW

O BURIAL CHAMBER

N

START

Walk 10

Mynydd Rhiw Circular

3 hours

This walk is quite a mixture, with pleasant country lanes and old houses, pretty scenery and mountain strolls. Quite a tiring walk but worth the effort.

Park where you can at the cottage called Pen-y-Groes, approximately 300 metres along the road from the crossroads in Rhiw village when heading towards Abersoch as there are no official parking places in the village, Map reference: SH 2284, 2777.

Take the road towards Rhiw crossroads and at these turn right heading through the village and past the post office, you will pass a house on the opposite side of the road to the post office called Rhiwenfa.[1]

Carry on to the next junction, bearing left at this.

In about 200 metres there is a road to your right and on the other side of the road, a stone stile, cross this and follow the footpath leading around the hillside.

This path carries on for about ½ a mile and passes through areas of old mine workings from the manganese mines.[2]

At the end of this section make towards the corner of the field and over the stone step stile in the drystone wall. Turn right here onto a green lane.[3]

Leave the green lane on the left after about 50 metres through a field gate and keeping to the wall on your left, head along this path until it approaches the road at a bend, unfortunately there is no stile here, so a spot of climbing may be necessary to get you onto the road. As a marker you will be about 90 degrees to the radio mast on Mynydd Rhiw.

155

Turn right onto the road and proceed along this for a fair distance, until the first right turn which will take you steadily uphill past a telephone box on your left and through a cluster of houses with fine views to your left.[4]•

Continue on up the hill, nearing the highest point on the road at the sign for the 'National Trust', opposite a large outcrop of rock, at this point if you would like a detour to the Neolithic axe factory on the eastern flanks of Mynydd Rhiw take the path up the hillside on your right and along the flank of the mountain can be seen some areas of loose stone, there are the remains of the axe factory.[5]

Retrace your steps to the road heading roughly in the direction of Rhiw with the large crescent of Porth Neigwl (*Hell's Mouth Bay*) sweeping into the distance.

After a short descent passing a cottage on the right called Heather, look for a lane leading off to the left with several names and post boxes including Tan-y-Gain, after turning into this lane make your way downhill until the lane passes some open ground on the left and on the right is an old farm without a name on the gate but is called Waen Cottage now, but on the Ordinance Survey map it is called Gwern Saer. Just after the cottage is a well, it is not named but is fairly large, about 3 metres square, continue along the path to the next cottage called Tan-y-Muriau. Just before you reach this cottage you will see on your right a long cairn or burial mound.[6]

Below the muriau is a sunken path, now overgrown, but you can walk beside it to the track, turn right and follow this path through a couple of gates until you emerge onto the road, turn right here and continue up hill passing on the way a house called Tyn-y-Graig.[7]

On reaching the 'T' Junction with the Rhiw — Sarn road at the church, turn left and follow this road back in to Rhiw. As you walk uphill look into the fields on your left just in front of a large white house where you will see the remains of another cromlech, similar, though not as large as the one just visited.[8]

Detour

As you reach the cottage Pen-y-Groes where you have parked your car and provided that you have a bit more energy left, carry on down the main road past the cottage on you left called Tan-y-Bwlch and turn left into a track next to a large white house called Llwynfor and beside the drive into the house is another lower one that leads into a field where just across the stream there is another long cairn or muriau, described later.

Retrace your steps to your car remembering to shut all gates.

History notes
[1] This house stands on the concrete that supported a tower holding the wheels that drove a cable lift system for moving manganese ore from a nearby mine — encountered shortly, down to the north west end of Hell's Mouth Bay to be loaded onto ships.

[2] The manganese mines visible here were worked at the same time and in conjunction with those at Nant-y-Gadwen (described in the last walk). There is a homestead settlement, the remains of which are visible with a little imagination, just the other side of the field wall at the end of the mine workings. There are field terracings which are associated with this hut group but they are virtually ploughed out. There are further terracings on the hillside, where there is also another hut circle, but thick gorse and heather now conceal them from view. The settlements here probably date from the Dark Age up to mediaeval times.

[3] On the rising spur of land to the left at this point is a concentric banked enclosure, the two banks form circles of 95 metres and 70 metres, they are only visible on the ground as slight swellings about 33 cms high and 3 metres wide. Locals recall removal of stones from these walls in recent years. A central feature is reputedly visible from air photographs and is probably the site of a dwelling. A writer in 1696 records a stone circle in this area and it is possible that this central feature represents the last trace of this. There is nothing else in the neighbourhood to which this description could apply. This double ring-work construction probably dates from the pre-Roman Iron Age c. 100 B.C., it is likely to be contemporary with other similar constructions on Llŷn e.g. Castell Caeron, Conion (both mentioned shortly), Pen-y-Gaer near Abersoch

visited in the first walk in this book.

[4] This section of closely associated small holdings is a fine example of the continuation of use into modern times of an area designated as a township possibly as early as the 12th century. The township was called 'Dindywydd'. The sites of the existing cottages are likely to be on the same sites as the original mediaeval dwellings. Two cottages remain with names harking back to this period, Brondywydd and Penydref (head of the township). There was a local tradition extant earlier in the present century that a disaster took place here. It seems that a love-lorn poet wandering in the area came to the township and asked for alms, he was refused and sent packing, he strongly resented this rebuttal and as he left he uttered a curse on the place which shortly after was destroyed by fire. Dindywydd was a 'bond vill' paying its dues and tributes to the 'maerdref' or 'Llys' of Neigwl (a maerdref or Llys is the dwelling place of the 'overlord' of the area). Just over the hill behind the house called 'Pen-y-Castell' is another concentric ring-work fort of Celtic date although virtually nothing now remains visible.

[5] The first farming communities reached Britain around 3500 B.C. in the Neolithic Age. Some of these people arrived by way of the Irish sea route and settled on the shores of Wales and Ireland. It is possible that the Neolithic period is as old on the Welsh coast as anywhere else in Britain. Very little remains as evidence of these early people in Llŷn except a few burial sites, some of which are quite impressive. There is however one other important site dating from the Neolithic — the stone-axe factory on the north-east slope of Mynydd Rhiw. This site was first recognised as an axe factory in 1956 when it was revealed by extensive gorse-burning. The site consists of five roughly circular hollows in a line about 90 metres long and bearing 40 degrees these hollows are the remains of an open cast mining system following a vein of suitable rock, the largest hollow at the north east end is about 15 metres across, the others vary between 4.5 metres and 7.5 metres across. The banks surrounding the hollows are composed of the waste product of flaking. It seems likely that the quarrying only took place in the

summer months, during the winter the people would have lived lower down the mountain side in a permanent community although nothing has been found to indicate where this may have been. It is possible that the factory workers may have lived on the site during the summer months as one of the hollows, on excavation showed evidence of two hearths. The date of these original workings may be as early as 3000 B.C. Two further hearths were discovered within the same hollow as the two previous but on a much higher level above the much silted-over earlier hearths, a tentative date in the 12th century B.C. has been assigned to the later hearths. This clearly shows that the factory was in use for many centuries and spanned the period of the Neolithic and early Bronze Ages. It is interesting that the later quarrying work seems to have been undertaken with less skill and attention to use of rock-type than the earlier.

Axe factories such as this (there are several around Britain) provide good evidence of an extensive and widespread trading system in this remote period, as tools produced at the various sites which are petrologically identifiable show up in widely dispersed regions. Tools from Mynydd Rhiw have been found all over Wales and the Marches, while those from another axe factory at Craig Lwyd, also in Caernarfonshire, near Llanfairfechan, have been found in Southern England and even on the Continent. This distribution implies a fairly advanced trading infrastructure. In the case of Mynydd Rhiw it appears that a range of tool-types were produced, including small delicate knives, scrapers, hand axes of various sizes, adzes and large tree-felling axes. Although trade has been established involving these products it may be that most of them were reserved for local use.

[6] This cromlech or 'long cairn' as it is more usually described, is, like the axe factory described above, of Neolithic date, indeed it is highly likely that it is the work of the same culture involved with the quarrying. The cromlech consists of a mound of loose stone about 27 metres long and 6 metres wide with a small ruined chamber at the North west end, and a larger chamber standing apart further to the North west. It is possible that the larger

Long Cairn

chamber was included in the mound of stones but that they have been removed to construct the field boundary. The structure can be visualised as consisting of two (or three) chambers containing burials with the whole covered by a mound of stones, there may have been a passage giving access to the interior of the mound on the South west side. This monument falls into the general class of 'chambered tombs', they are present, often with characteristic regional differences throughout the whole of Britain. They demonstrate the almost universally similar burial customs of the peoples inhabiting Britain in the Neolithic period. Although these structures are generally considered to be funerary monuments it is quite likely that they had a wider role in the community. In fact it may be helpful to consider them as having a similar function to a church. The church, for us, as well as being a place of burial, is also a place of worship, it is often a communal centre and focus, a source of communal pride, a place of security and sanctuary, the sacred ground of the community. The Neolithic cromlech's and passage graves were undoubtedly the most permanent and impressive buildings, with by far the most effort and man-hours invested in them — they are still with us 5000 years after their construction. It would seem then that these monuments had a deep awe inspiring religious significance, and a little imagination at this site can conjure up a scene with the silent members of the community witnessing the ritual internment of a beloved chief, a moving ceremony performed by the tribal shaman who would wait, maybe with a few of the chief's close relatives, for the time of sunset, and when it dips close to the horizon, and the hillside is bathed in ruddy gold, the spirit of the dead chief rises and leaves its earthly tomb through the open south-west passage to greet his ancestors once again and walk in splendour behind the setting sun.

Tyn-y-Graig

[7] Tyn-y-Graig — this cottage, built in 1762 (there is an inscription cut into the face of the east wall: WWI/1762, probably for William Williams, the owner and his wife who in 1776 lived at Plas-yn-Rhiw). There is reason to believe that, in spite of the date inscription that the house is earlier, say early 18th century, this evidence comes from the plan and the nature and quality of

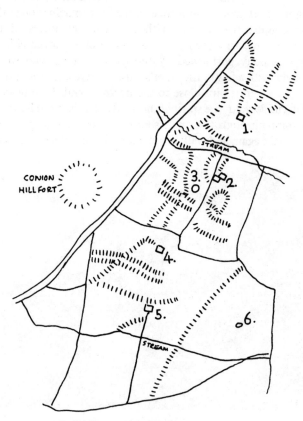

FIG. 2.

HUTS AND FIELD SYSTEMS AT RHIW.

construction of the woodwork inside. The house today retains almost all of its character, it is nice to see an old Welsh cottage neither derelict, nor 'modernised' out of all recognition.

[8] In the sloping field to the left of the road at this point is another complex system of huts and fields and it is proposed to give a diagram with explanatory notes as was done for a similar system in the last walk. (See Fig. 2)

1. This is the remains of a long hut 9.4 metres long x 5.2 metres wide, the walls are 30cm high and the south west wall shows a 1 metre wide entrance.

2. Long hut, 100 metres South-west of (1) 8 metres long x 5 metres wide, the walls are now just grassy banks with an occasional stone visible, there is a similar sized and shaped enclosure adjoining it on the same axis, this was probably a 'yard'.

3. A circular platform 6 metres in diameter, probably the site of a round hut.

4. Ruins of a house 5.75 metres x 3.3 metres probably on the site of a former long hut.

5. Site of long hut ruined by construction of modern wall 60 metres S.S.W. of (4).

Surrounding these features are numerous remains of contemporary field boundaries (see accompanying diagram).

As has been mentioned before, these long huts may be of a later date than the round huts. If, for sake of argument, the round hut systems are dated to the late-Roman period and early Dark Ages c.400-700 A.D. it may be that the long huts represent the period of the later Dark Ages c.700-1100 A.D. It cannot be emphasised too often that it is impossible to be accurate with dates for huts in general and these dates are only intended to be a guide.

Burial chamber

6. Burial chamber, a similar though less imposing construction
than the one described above, nevertheless, dates from the same
period, it may have been earth-covered rather than stone-covered.
There has been an attempt made in the past to destroy this site by
blasting (note the holes drilled in the large capstone) and two slabs
10 metres to the south of the site may have been removed from the
monument. See detour at end of walk.

There is another ring-work fort of the pre-Roman Celtic period a
few metres to the right of the road on top of a small hill, it is called
'Conion', nothing is visible from the road and the fort is in a poor
state of preservation. A 'rotary quern' was found here in 1960.

Walks with History
Walks in the Llŷn Peninsula
Part 2
by Nigel Burras and Jeff Stiff

If you have enjoyed the walks described in this book, or if you are an 'armchair walker' and have enjoyed reading some of the varied history of the area contained in the historical notes, then look out for the second book of the series, which has a further ten walks centred around the superb mountain and coastal scenery on the north-eastern side of the peninsula, around the villages of Nefyn, Morfa Nefyn and Edern.